Clayton P. Fisher

The Stock Market

Explained

For Young Investors

Business Classics
Woodside, California 94062

Business Classics
950 Purisima
Woodside, California 94062

Copyright © Clayton P. Fisher 1993

This publication is designed to provide accurate and authoritative information in regard to the subject matter covered. It is sold with the understanding that the publisher is not engaged in rendering legal, accounting, or other professional service. If legal or other expert assistance is required, the service of a competent professional person should be sought.

From the Declaration of Principles jointly adopted by a Committee of the American Bar Association and a Committee of Publishers.

ISBN   0-931133-02-5

Printed in the United States of America
     2   3   4   5   6   7   8   9   10

**For young investors who
have caught stock market fever!**

Acknowledgments

Some people think acknowledgments are silly. I used to. But after seeing all the work that so many people put into this book, I feel a need to thank them -- without them I would never have been able to write this book.

First and foremost I give thanks to my father, Ken Fisher, who came up with the idea for this book and whose guidance and tutelage blew life into this book's lungs. Huge thanks also go to my mother, Sherri Fisher, whose skills in marketing and publishing made this book happen. I owe Craig Braemer, former Head of Research for Fisher Investments and currently its Chief Financial Officer, for a substantial portion of my stock market education, out of which this book grew.

There are so many people left to thank that I hope those I don't thank here will forgive me. Thanks to Colin Barrows, the Brothers of Sigma Chi, and my two favorite people, Nathan & Jesse, my little brothers. Special thanks to my grandparents for their input and especially my grandfather, Phil Fisher, who's guilty of giving me stock market fever.

Table of Contents

INTRODUCTION

About four years ago, a client of my father's asked him if he knew of any good books about the stock market for his 18-year-old son. My father hadn't heard of one. His response was "No, but my son could write one." At the time I was just shy of seventeen.

The goal was not to write a book like *How to Buy Stocks*. A guy named Louis Engel wrote that book and it's probably the best at explaining all the ins and outs of buying and selling stocks. But most young investors wouldn't want to start out with that book--it's about 350 pages long and isn't geared for young people.

The goal of my book is to give a young person a sense of what investing is all about. It does this by first briefly explaining different investments, where they are traded, why they go up and down, and why a young person would be interested. It then explains in simple terms the economics behind the market, what indexes like the Dow really are, some accounting

1

you need to know in order to invest, different ways to value companies, and how a young investor might investigate those companies. It explains the different strategies the pros use and shows how, with a few simple rules, young investors can use largely the same strategies and stay safe, too. The last chapter is a collection of brief descriptions about books by authors who are among the best investors of all time. It is designed to lead you anywhere you're interested.

Your natural reaction might be that all this stuff is too complicated and boring for you. **Bull! You can do it.** Most financial people would like you to believe it's too hard for most folks to understand because it makes what they do seem really tough. But the simple truth is the wide world of stocks is not really that hard to understand. All through school I have been plagued by textbooks with such awful language that my first reaction is often: "This must be hard to understand because I can't even 'get' the first sentence." But after struggling through the entire book and falling asleep who knows how many times, I usually find the stuff in the book wasn't all that hard to understand after all. Fact is, if the books were written in a language more like English, I would have understood them in a flash.

Well, financial books have the same rep. Some folks say drugstores should sell financial books to their customers instead of sleeping pills. Not my book, damn it!!! Part of the challenge was to write a financial book guaranteed to keep a young person awake!

That included several things. First, the book is not in small print. If your eyes hurt from looking at small print, you are bound to close them. Next, only about one in 10 financial books has charts, and only about 1 in 20 has pictures, and most of those have only one or two. *Playboy's Investment and Financial Guide for Singles* doesn't even have any pictures in it. Don't get me wrong--I'm not trying to insult your intelligence by making this a picture book. But it is nice to be able to see what you are reading about--you might even stay interested, heaven forbid. But for how long? Very few young people or maybe even sane people want to read a 1000-page Bible about the stock market. That's why this book is relatively short--it's designed to get you all the way through. Last and most importantly, to keep you awake, unlike most financial books, the book has to be in a language you are used to, like young people's English. I hope when you are reading this book it seems as if I'm right there talking to you.

CHAPTER 1

YOU MIGHT BE INTERESTED!!!

Do you know someone who works in the investment industry--or maybe someone who owns lots of stock? Maybe your parents, an uncle, or an older brother or sister? Have you ever been asked what they do? Do you know? Have some of their conversations gone right over your head? Would you like to know what they're talking about? More importantly, would you like to know what they do? In one short book you can learn enough to understand what they do and what they're talking about and maybe even have some fun and make a little money.

High Paying Careers

Lots of people in the investment industry make big bucks. For example: David Dreman sold 80% of his business for $100 million. Before that he was probably making somewhere between $15-$20 million a year. Dozens of owners of investment management firms make as much or more.

Then there are stockbrokers. There are literally dozens of brokers who gross $5,000,000 per year in commissions. They're taking home about $2,500,000 per year in net income. There are thousands of brokers who bring in $100,000 and up every year.

Exciting Careers

A job in the investment industry can be one of the most fun and exciting jobs going. As I write, Delta stock is plummeting because one of their planes just crashed in Dallas. You can be on the scene, too. One morning I woke up, walked downstairs into my Dad's investment management firm, and found that Borland International had made an offer to buy one of my stocks--Ashton-Tate--for $17.50 per share; the stock was up five bucks as soon as the market opened. There are always things happening-- like a proxy fight or a takeover--and there's an intensity in the air that excites everyone. The investment industry is loaded with action. It's not just your average "sit behind the desk and be bored" kind of job.

Getting Ahead

How can you prepare yourself for a job in the investment industry? Read this book! It's designed to get you ahead. By getting ahead, you'll be able to learn more later. You make yourself more attractive to future employers and you'll be worth more to them when you start working. By getting ahead in your knowledge of the investment industry, you put yourself ahead. My dad started working for his dad when he was very young. By the time he was 23, he was a practicing investment manager. Today, at 42 he's more successful than most people his age because he got an early start.

Understand How The U.S. Works

The U.S. economy is a very complicated thing. There are tons of reasons why things happen. It's important to understand how and why things work. Do you understand capitalism? Everyone knows that in capitalist economies people own the businesses. But how could **you** own IBM? The stock market is the answer. Through it, millions of individuals can own tiny parts of any business they want. If you understand how this works, you'll have a much better understanding of capitalism and why it's the world's most efficient economic system.

Self-Reliance

My friends and I were really worried about taking the SAT. We were also worried about getting into the "right college." One common thought is: "Can I cut it in the real world?" We hear the words, "It's natural to be a little insecure about your life when you are young." One reason young people are insecure is because they don't get many chances to prove themselves in the real world. You probably don't get the chance to do the same things for work as your parents. You might get a part-time job doing some no-brain work, or maybe if you're strong you have a construction job doing manual labor for $9 an hour. But few young people get big chances to prove themselves in the real world.

The stock market is one way to prove yourself and build your self-reliance. **You** can invest! The market doesn't care how young you are, and the stock you own never knows. The market acts the same way for you as it does for a 75-year-old. You can take the money you've earned from a part-time job and test your skill in the market. Or, if you don't feel ready after reading this book, you could play-invest. Just choose your stocks--follow them --and learn without using your money. Follow the stock prices in the newspaper. At first this step might be best just in case you get in over your head. Even if you mess up, which is inevitable, you can learn from your mistakes --at least when you're play-investing your first (and often your biggest) mistakes will be pain-less.

Money

Most people are interested in the stock market because it's a great place to make bucks. That's true. It is a place where people make and lose bundles. Some people think making money in the stock market is an easy thing to do. The opportunities exist. You need to be able to take advantage of them. Investing can make you lots of money if you do it right. My grandfather used to ask, "What's the best way to end up with $1,000,000 in the stock market?" The answer--"Start out with $2,000,000." Lots of people lose money in the stock market because they don't invest wisely. If you invest wisely--which isn't a hard thing to learn to do --you can make a million starting out with very little. Honestly. How? **Keep reading!!!**

Compound Interest

Few people know the awesome "power of compound interest." If they knew, there would be millionaires everywhere. It's not hard to make a million bucks in the market. It doesn't happen overnight, but it's really easy. Here's how!

For the last 60 years, the 500 companies in the Standard and Poor's 500 have returned 9% to 10% compounded per year for investors. What does compounding money mean? It's <u>earning interest on both an investment and the interest that investment pays</u>. Wow, take a breath and read the last sentence again if it didn't register. Suppose you put $1,000 in a bank

After	Started		Yearly		New
The	With	+	Interest	=	Total
1st Year	$1,000.00	+	$50.00	=	$1,050.00
2nd Year	$1,050.00	+	$52.50	=	$1,102.50
3rd Year	$1,102.50	+	$55.07	=	$1,155.57
4th Year	$1,155.57	+	$57.79	=	$1,211.36
5th Year	$1,211.36	+	$60.57	=	$1,271.93
6th Year	$1,271.93	+	$63.60	=	$1,335.53
7th Year	$1,335.53	+	$66.78	=	$1,402.31
8th Year	$1,402.31	+	$71.12	=	$1,472.43
9th Year	$1,472.31	+	$73.62	=	$1,545.93
10th Year	$1,545.93	+	$77.30	=	$1,623.23
15th Year	$1,979.93	+	$99.00	=	$2,078.93
25th Year	$3,225.10	+	$161.25	=	$3,386.35
35th Year	$5,253.35	+	$262.67	=	$5,516.02
50th Year	$10,921.33	+	$546.07	=	$11,487.40

paying about 5%. Let's see what happens over the years when you leave your interest in the bank.

If you took your interest out at every year-end, you would have your original $1,000 plus 50 years worth of $50 interest payments --amounting to $3,500 total ($1,000 + (50 X $50) = $3,500.) But, compounding your money,

11

according to the chart, gives you $11,487.40. Wow! Earning interest on interest, as well as

After The	Started With	+	Yearly Interest	=	New Total
1st Year	$1,000	+	$100	=	$1,100
2nd Year	$1,100	+	$110	=	$1,210
3rd Year	$1,210	+	$121	=	$1,331
4th Year	$1,331	+	$133	=	$1,464
5th Year	$1,464	+	$146	=	$1,610
6th Year	$1,610	+	$161	=	$1,771
7th Year	$1,771	+	$177	=	$1,948
8th Year	$1,948	+	$194	=	$2,143
9th Year	$2,143	+	$214	=	$2,357
10th Year	$2,357	+	$235	=	$2,593
15th Year	$3,797	+	$379	=	$4,177
25th Year	$9,849	+	$984	=	$10,834
35th Year	$25,547	+	$2,554	=	$28,102
50th Year	$106,718	+	$10,671	=	$117,390

your original investment, works like magic.

If we double the interest rate to 10%, will we finish with $22,974.80?

Wow, $117,390.86! Like before, if you take the interest out at every year-end, you'd have only $7,000 in 50 years. But, by compounding your money at 10%, you'd get $117,390.86! That's the power of compound interest. Making interest on interest works like magic.

By using compound interest, everyone can make a million in time to use it. It requires some discipline, but you could do it. If, starting at age 25, you invested $2,000 per year at 10% in a tax-free Individual Retirement Account (IRA), by the time you were 65, you'd have a million bucks. It's not hard to make a million bucks in the market--it just takes time.

But there's more. Suppose you did better than 10%. If you compound $10,000 at 20%, you'd be a millionaire in only 25 years. If you compound $10,000 at 25%, you'd have a million bucks in 20 years and a billion bucks in 52 years. People have done it. Warren Buffett is the most famous. He made $3.5 billion from almost nothing and is now a legend. So, if you want to learn how to make a million in time to use it--read on--and get an early start.

CHAPTER 2

SOME BASICS

On May 17th, 1792, 24 New York City merchants joined forces to trade the public's stock on Wall Street--outside, under a buttonwood tree. Initially, trading was limited to government, bank, and insurance company securities. The first investors resisted buying stock. They thought they'd lose their money. By 1793, the exchange grew enough to move

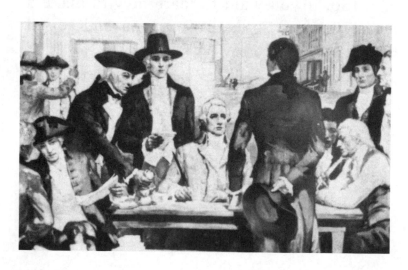

to an inside location at Tontine Coffee House on the corner of Wall and William Streets, about a block from its present site.

Later the volume and the number of investors skyrocketed. In 1863, the exchange moved to its present site--Wall Street--and in 1886 celebrated its first million share day. Today a million shares trade each morning in the first five minutes. Even more impressive was the incredible 600 million share volume during October 1987's big crash.

Tontine Coffee House

Organizational Structure

Business ownership falls into four groups:

- Sole-Proprietorship
- General Partnership
- Limited Partnership
- Corporate

We will review these kinds of businesses. But because we are interested in stocks, we will concentrate on corporations. However, you should understand other business forms, too.

1) **Sole-Proprietorship**

Sole-proprietorship, in plain English, means "one owner." Businesses owned and run by one person are usually smaller--not the General Motors of the world. Bill's Bar-B-Q is a likely name for a sole-proprietorship. Bill owns and runs his country-style restaurant. All profits (sales minus expenses) and losses go to Bill. The government taxes Bill's profits, or income, like an individual, separate from his restaurant. "Liability" is a problem with sole-proprietorships. If Bill's Bar-B-Q is sued because an employee accidentally poisons a customer, Bill is being sued and he is responsible. Bill's home, car, and other assets are on the line.

2) General Partnership

In a general partnership, two or more people join to manage a business under an agreement--usually a contract--stating:

- What the business does
- How long the partnership will last
- How the profits are divided
- What each partner does
- How much money (or capital) each partner brings to the business initially

Each partner is taxed individually on the profit or income he/she receives as specified in the contract. New partners can't join without agreement from the other partners. Usually, partners are equally responsible for business debts. However, if a general partnership goes bankrupt and its debts need to be paid, creditors can collect from any partner who has money. So, richer partners can lose more. For example, if your dad's partner caused huge liabilities, creditors could take your family's home and savings as payment for your dad's partner's screw-up.

3) Limited Partnership

Limited partnerships are like general partnerships but have both general partners and "limited" partners. The general partners are the same as in general partnerships; limited partners are different. Limited partners get a share of business profits and losses but aren't responsible for business management. It's called a limited partnership because the limited partner is "limited" in liability to the money he/she initially invested (capital). If your dad is a limited partner, he can only lose his original investment if other partners screw up.

4) Corporate

A corporation's structure is unlike other businesses'. The key point to remember is: shareholders own companies. Why? When a company is founded, shareholders put down money (capital) for the company's assets and maintenance. Unlike sole-proprietors or general partners, corporate shareholders aren't responsible for business debts. To form a corporation, incorporators (usually three) submit to their state an application for a charter containing:

- A thorough description of the business
- The corporation's title
- The names of the incorporators
- The number of shares and par value of the common stock and possibly preferred stock (if the company chooses)

The corporation (or company) is born. Corporations must issue shares. Why? Corporations need money to function and grow. By selling shares, corporations raise money. When corporations are young, shares are sold to private parties--usually individuals. Founders, people who submitted an application for a charter, usually buy the initial stock. What if a couple of shareholders wanted to sell the stock? They'd have to sell the stock privately to someone. They'd have to know someone who wanted to buy it. Chances are they don't. It's a big world. They need help! They'd go to an investment banking firm. This firm specializes in making stock available to the public and distributing it. The Initial Public Offering (or IPO) is, as the name sounds, the first time the stock is offered to the public. From there on out anyone can buy and sell the stock.

The board of directors is chosen by stockholders. The board of directors appoints officers. Officers manage the company. The company, by the charter, is a legal entity in itself. It's completely separate from directors and officers. It can sue and be sued in its own name, like a person. Corporations also have advantages which allow them to grow; they can borrow large amounts of money or they can sell additional stock.

Four O.K. Securities

There are four securities young people should stick to. These are common securities issued by corporations and governments:

- Common Stock
- Corporate and Treasury Bonds

- Money Market Funds (cash equivalents)
- Mutual Funds

These are the basics. Most professionals, who manage billions of dollars, stick to these securities when trading for clients. These are the only securities beginning investors should consider.

1) **Common Stock**

Stocks are traded at marketplaces called exchanges. Common stocks have privileges. Common stockholders are owners and theoretically have 1 vote per share. If a stockholder owns 50% of a company, he/she controls it. Common stockholders, through directors and managers, control companies.

Privileges cost. Because common stockholders control companies, it's assumed that if there are problems it's the common shareholders' fault. So, if companies go bankrupt and sell their assets to raise money to pay off debts, common stockholders are paid last. Conversely, when companies make money they can do two things: they can use it to grow by buying more assets (like factories, machines,

100 Shares of Filenet Corporation

or offices) or they can give it to shareholders. When companies have profits and divide them equally among shareholders, these divided profits are called dividends. Companies pay dividends only when they have unused profits or past accumulated earnings.

2) **Corporate and Treasury Bonds**

Buying bonds is like putting money in an inflexible savings account. <u>When you put money in the bank you're giving the bank a loan</u>. Banks use your money to make themselves more money. They pay interest for the use of your money. <u>Interest is the cost of borrowing money. When buying a bond you're making the issuer of the bond a loan</u>. Bond issuers pay bond owners an interest rate for the use of their money. Since interest rates change as time passes, the interest rates of newly-issued bonds change. Bonds pay higher interest rates than bank accounts because they're riskier and less flexible.

Bond interest can be paid two ways: by coupon or automatically. "Coupon bonds" come with a specified number of coupons. Periodically, you mail in a coupon and receive the interest payment for the time period. When a coupon bond reaches maturity (the end of its life), whoever holds it gets paid the bond's face value. So, if you lose a coupon bond with a $1,000 face value, it's like losing $1,000 cash. Coupon bonds are becoming less common.

Fully registered bonds' interest payments are kept track of by the issuer at his/her expense. The issuer or his/her bank makes regular payments to bond owners. This is convenient for bond owners, but makes fully registered bonds pay slightly lower interest rates than coupon bonds. A fully registered bondholder gets certificates carrying his/her name, the bond's face value, and interest rate. Fully registered bonds are the most common.

At a bond's initial offering, the seller chooses when the bond's face value will be repaid--its **maturity**. It's called maturity because it's when the bond comes of age. Issuers have to pay higher interest rates for long-term bonds because longer term loans mean more risk for the lender. At maturity, bond issuers pay owners the face value (the bond's initial cost--its **par value**). Bond owners have no responsibility for the issuer's other liabilities and debts. Bonds are debts, and if issuers can't pay, bond owners have first dibs on the issuer's assets--even before stockholders. If there aren't enough assets to repay bond owners in full, bond owners lose the difference. So there are risks with bonds.

There are three standard bonds. Young investors should bother with only two--Treasury bonds and corporate bonds. As the names suggest, Treasury bonds are issued by the U.S. Treasury and corporate bonds are issued by corporations. The government pays only slightly higher interest rates than banks because the government is a very safe investment. Companies, on the other hand, issue bonds whose interest rates vary with the bond's risk of default (bankruptcy). Larger companies with little risk of default pay lower interest rates than smaller, more risky companies. Bonds of larger companies are still slightly more risky than government bonds--because even the Texacos of the world can go bankrupt. Since smaller companies go bankrupt more easily, they must pay more to entice people to buy their bonds. Some extremely risky companies pay outrageously high interest rates on bonds. These bonds are called "junk bonds."

3) **Money Market Funds**

Investors often have cash and want to have it invested in high-paying liquid securities (easily sold for cash--doesn't tie up money for long periods). The best short-term securities that pay high interest rates are cash equivalents. A cash equivalent (or a security almost as liquid as cash) is a **Short-term Bond** lasting usually for 30 to 270 days. Cash equivalents pay lower interest rates than long-term bonds because borrowers would rather borrow money longer and short-term bonds are safer. They also have a higher par value because it usually takes huge amounts of money to make it worthwhile for the issuer to issue the bond. Some cash equivalents are: Commercial Paper, Certificates of Deposit, and short-term Treasury Bills. We'll talk more about them later.

Money Market Funds buy and sell these cash equivalents for their clients. By trading cash for cash equivalents you might say money market funds "make a market for money." When investors bring money to money market funds, everyone's money is pooled into one big account. Each owner has a share of the pool. By pooling money together, owners of money market fund shares can indirectly purchase large cash equivalents that they wouldn't be able to buy individually. The fund earns the average fund interest rate minus a management fee. Each individual investor has an account, like a bank account, with the fund. Most money market funds allow investors to write checks from their accounts and take money out whenever they want.

4) **Mutual Funds**

Mutual funds are just like money market funds except mutual funds can buy and sell not only cash equivalents, but anything they specify. There are mutual funds that buy different kinds of stocks, bonds, and real estate. If you don't want to buy your own stocks, you can buy shares in a mutual fund. Mutual funds are a pretty safe place for your money because they stay diversified.

So why only these? Well, common stocks, corporate and Treasury bonds, money

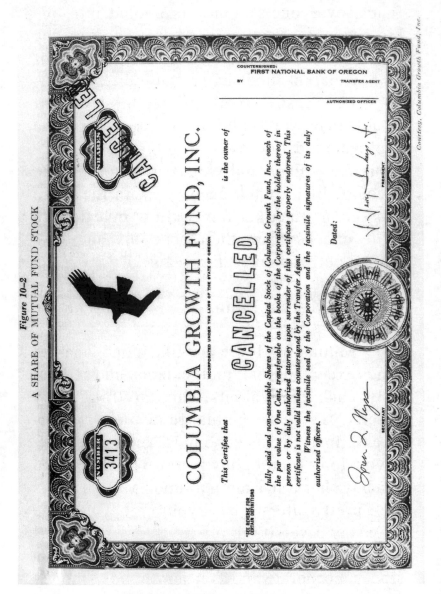

Figure 10-2

A SHARE OF MUTUAL FUND STOCK

Courtesy, Columbia Growth Fund, Inc.

Mutual Fund Shares

market funds, and mutual funds are safer securities for young people. Later, we will examine these investments further. Right now we will concentrate on **investments you shouldn't use**, but should know about--sort of like drugs. You could use them, but it's likely they will hurt you more than help you. There are six:

- Preferred Stock
- Municipal Bonds
- Commercial Paper
- Certificates of Deposit
- Puts and Calls
- Convertible Bonds

1) **Preferred Stock**

Preferred stock is like a cross between common stock and corporate bonds; it has characteristics of a stock, but it trades like a bond. "Preferred stock" is a misnomer--that is, it is improperly named. Preferred stock has "safety" advantages, but also has severe restrictions common stock doesn't have. Preferred stock doesn't have common stock's upward potential; preferred stock probably won't rise like common stock, but it can fall to zero.

Companies often have the right to buy their own preferred stock back at a certain price (this right is called a "Call"). For shareholders who want a stock to fly through the roof, this is a raw deal.

The preferred stockholder has no vote in the company's management. If companies go bankrupt, fault is assumed to lie with the common shareholders who voted for the bad management. In bankruptcy, preferred shareholders have rights to liquidated assets before common shareholders. If dividends are paid, preferred stockholders get fixed dividends like a bond's interest rate. When companies don't pay dividends to preferred shareholders, any unpaid dividends are paid in full before common stockholders get any dividends. We invest for the return on our money. Curbed or restricted stocks, even with large dividends, are unlikely to do as well as uncurbed common stocks.

2) Municipal Bonds

Municipal bonds are issued by a municipality. A municipality is a group from a state, city, town, or even a school district. These groups sell municipal bonds to raise money to fund the building of schools, bridges, dams, parks, police departments, city halls, fire departments, and even roads. Municipal bonds pay lower interest rates than corporate or government bonds because the interest income is tax-free. For people who pay lots of taxes, tax-free bonds are a better deal than many corporate bonds with higher interest rates. Most young people don't pay lots of taxes. Tax-free bonds that pay lower interest rates will earn young people less than taxed bonds at higher interest rates.

3) **Commercial Paper and**
4) **Certificates of Deposit**

These securities are cash equivalents. They are large short-term bonds. Usually the length of these bonds is 30 to 270 days, as specified when they are issued. Corporations sell commercial paper. Banks issue certificates of deposit. Both of these cash equivalents usually sell for at least $100,000. If they cost less than $100,000, they will probably pay significantly lower interest rates. Because few young people have $100,000, these securities aren't practical.

5) **Puts and Calls** (options)

"Puts" are dangerous! Buying a put option is buying "the right to sell" a stock at a certain price at a later date. "Calls" and puts are opposites. When buying a call you're buying "the right to buy" stock at a certain price and date in the future. You're hoping the price goes up! Calls generally cost more than puts because the market goes up more than it goes down. Puts and calls expire at varied times--usually one month to a year. Puts and calls are very risky. To make money on puts or calls you must get a stock to move several dollars, in the favorable direction, in a short time. This is unlikely; it's mostly luck when it happens!

Options cost! Why would anyone pay to be able to do this? Let's say you bought a put on XYZ common stock. The price option sellers will give you for XYZ at, on, or before the expiration date is $80 per share. Let's say you want a two-month option. This option might cost $3 per share or $300 for an option on 100 shares. You want the price to go down! If the price drops from $80 to $66 1/2, and you exercise the option, you will make a bundle.

LOMBARD STREET INC.

Members Put and Call Brokers and Dealers Association, Inc.

PUT AND CALL OPTIONS

GUARANTEED BY MEMBERS N.Y. STOCK EXCHANGE

170 BROADWAY, N.Y. 10038   349-7145

No. 2204

EXPIRES
3:15 P.M.,
NEW YORK, N.Y. TIME

February 10   19 70

SOLD BY MEMBER
PUT & CALL
BROKERS & DEALERS
ASSOCIATION Inc.

Copr. 1957, Put and Call Brokers and Dealers Assn., Inc.

For Value Received, the BEARER may CALL on the endorser for ONE HUNDRED (100) shares of the stock of the

ABC Corporation (ABC)

at—

Twenty-eight   Dollars ($28.00)   per share

ANY TIME WITHIN

six months and ten days   days from date.

New York, N.Y.   July 31   1969   common

THIS STOCK OPTION CONTRACT MUST BE PRESENTED, AS SPECIFIED BELOW, TO THE ENDORSING FIRM BEFORE THE EXPIRATION OF THE EXACT TIME LIMIT. IT CANNOT BE EXERCISED BY TELEPHONE.

DURING THE LIFE OF THIS OPTION:

1. (a) — the contract price hereof shall be reduced by the value of any cash dividend on the day the stock goes ex-dividend;
(b) — where the Option is entitled to rights and/or warrants the contract price shall be reduced by the value of same as fixed by the opening sale thereof on the day the stock sells ex-rights and/or ex-warrants;
2. (a) — in the event of stock splits, reverse splits or other similar action by the above-mentioned corporation, this Option shall become an Option for the equivalent number of shares that are duly limited for trading and the total contract price shall not be reduced;
(b) — stock dividends or the equivalent due-bills shall be attached to the stock covered hereby, when and if this Option is exercised, and the total contract price shall not be reduced.
3. The exercise of this Option is subject to and governed by the By-Laws, Rules, Rulings and Regulations of the Put and Call Brokers and Dealers Association, Inc.

Upon presentation of the endorser of this Option attached to a comparison ticket in the manner and time specified, the endorser agrees to accept notice of the Bearer's exercise by stamping the comparison, and this acknowledgment shall constitute a contract and shall be controlling with respect to delivery of the stock and settlement in accordance with New York Stock Exchange usage.

The undersigned acts as intermediary only, without obligation other than to obtain a New York Stock Exchange firm as Endorser.

Lombard Street Inc.

CALL OPTION

Copr. 1957, Put and Call Brokers and Dealers Assn., Inc.

For Value Received, the BEARER may DELIVER to the endorser ONE HUNDRED (100) shares of the stock of the

XYZ Corporation (XYZ)

Seventy-five   Dollars ($75.00)   per share

six months and ten days   days from date.

New York, N.Y.   July 31   1969   common

...MUST BE PRESENTED, AS SPECIFIED BELOW, TO THE ENDORSING FIRM BEFORE THE

...MUST BE EXERCISED BY TELEPHONE.

349-7145

PUT OPTION

A Put and a Call Option

To exercise the put, you must buy 100 shares of XYZ at $66 1/2 per share, costing $6,650. The broker's commission for XYZ stock costs roughly $50 and the option costs $300, making your total cost $7,000. But, you'll receive $8,000 from the option seller for the 100 shares of XYZ, leaving you with $1000. If the stock goes up, the option would expire and you'd lose $300 (the option's cost). Chances are, in short periods, XYZ doesn't move. This is why most people who invest in options lose money.

6) Convertible Bonds

Convertibles are even more complicated than Puts and Calls. For example, say you buy a convertible bond at $1,000, or par value (the original cost of the bond when issued). This convertible pays a coupon, or fixed interest rate, of say 10%. So far, convertibles sound like regular old bonds. However, convertibles give you the option to exchange the bond for a specified number of common shares. Initially our convertible's stock value is below its bond value--at about $800. If the stock goes up, we could exercise the option (by converting the bond to stock), sell the stock, and make a nice profit. Like other options you don't have to exercise it. If you don't exercise it, you will always have the convertible's bond value. Before using convertibles you should be an experienced option, stock, and bond investor. We'll stick to simpler securities!

CHAPTER 3

HOW THE STOCK
MARKET WORKS

To understand how the stock market works, let's follow a trade from beginning to end. There are many investments beginning investors needn't use. One reason for this is because there are so many investments--literally jillions. Our trade will concern itself only with important areas for beginners.

The Investment Professional

Company XYZ has 10,000 employees. The company puts money in a pension plan to pay employees back when they retire so they'll have money to support themselves. Companies want to invest the money so their pension plans will grow enough to support employees in the future. Company XYZ makes widgets and that's all. They don't know a whole lot about investing, so they decide to hire some-one who specializes in investments to do the job for them. They hire an investment profes-sional, otherwise known as an Investment or Portfolio Manager.

About 85% of all the trading on the New York Stock Exchange is done by investment managers. Most of the money gets invested by investment managers. They manage money for wealthy individuals, insurance companies, banks, mutual funds, and pension funds. Most of the money managed by investment profes-sionals is pension money. Portions of pension funds from government agencies and corpora-tions are allotted to managers. Investment managers usually receive a percentage of mon-ies they handle--generally between .4% and 2%.

You, the individual investor, also force the mighty investment wheel to turn--it all starts with you. Deciding to invest is the first step. Suppose you like Ford Motor Company and want to buy 100 shares. You call your broker and place an order. If you don't have a broker, you'd call a brokerage firm and set up an account with the firm and broker.

The Broker

Stockbrokers are employed by broker-age houses--firms set up to help brokers trade. Brokers take orders and place them with their trader, who trades the stock. Brokers must pass a test administered by the Stock Exchange. This test is like the lawyer's bar exam except it's not as hard. Brokers are salespeople, like real estate agents or life insurance salespersons who make money from commissions. Stockbrokers keep a percentage of their commissions--usually between 25% and 50%. Commissions vary with trade size. Bigger trades mean bigger commissions; when brokers sell more, they make more. This way, better brokers can be paid more. Most brokerage houses have a minimum commission, or a minimum "ticket." If Dean Witter has a $30 minimum ticket, even if you want to buy two shares you have to pay them $30 to do it.

Round and Odd Lots

Most stocks are traded in round lots, or 100-share denominations. Brokers like round lots because they're easy to track and they give nice commissions. "Odd lots" are trades of less than 100 shares. Because odd lot trades are small, numerous, and hard to track, their commissions are higher, compared to total cost, than round lots. Most people buy stock in round lots.

The Brokerage House

There are different brokerage houses for different jobs. Retail brokerage houses are the most common. These firms give personalized information and services to individual investors. Institutional firms trade for investment managers who require less personal attention. The biggest firms have both retail and institutional departments. Over-the-Counter firms specialize in trading stock from broker to broker. They don't usually trade through the exchanges. Odd-Lot firms specialize in, yes, buying and selling odd lots. Specialist firms trade stock in a few companies for their accounts. They have specialists on exchange floors to make trades. The specialist's job is to keep prices stable.

When your broker, probably from a retail investment firm, has your Ford order, he wires it directly to the exchange floor where a trader picks it up. Brokerage houses buy "seats" on exchange floors for their traders. In earlier days, the New York Stock Exchange existed in large rented buildings and each broker had a seat from which to trade. Only brokers with seats (and their support staffs) were allowed in the exchange. Today brokers don't trade from seats, but the word "seat" is used to describe exchange membership. Seats (or memberships) are very expensive. In 1929, a seat sold for $625,000. There are about 1400 seats on the New York Stock Exchange. There are many different exchanges:

- NYSE (The New York Stock Exchange)
- OTC (The Over-the-Counter Market)
- ASE (The American Stock Exchange)
- Regional Exchanges

1) **The New York Stock Exchange-- NYSE**

The New York Stock Exchange, the largest U.S. exchange, is on Wall Street, New York City. About 80% of U.S. trades are done on the NYSE. Your Ford trade will probably go through the NYSE. Other exchange prices follow NYSE prices. The NYSE opens at 9:30 a.m. Eastern time (or 6:30 Pacific time) and closes at 4 p.m. Eastern time (or 1:00 p.m. Pacific time).

The New York Stock Exchange

2) **The Over-The-Counter Market-- OTC**

The second largest market isn't an exchange, it's the Over-the-Counter (OTC) market. The over-the-counter market isn't a place. The OTC trades from one brokerage house to another, swapping among each other, buying and selling for their own accounts, as well as for you. The market is a network of brokers' computers called NASDAQ--National Association of Securities Dealers Automated Quotes. To trade OTC stocks brokers use NASDAQ, which lists all brokerage firms trading the stocks and the price they want for their stock. Brokers trade stock with whatever brokerage firm has the best offer. Most banks and insurance companies are traded over-the-counter; some are too small to be listed on the NYSE. OTC stocks can be traded on other exchanges. About one out of 10 trades is done OTC.

3) The American Stock Exchange--ASE

For decades, the OTC market wasn't very good. Back then the American Stock Exchange was the second largest exchange. It's a national exchange like the NYSE, located in New York

City. The ASE trades more foreign securities than any other U.S. exchange. A stock listed on the ASE won't be listed on the NYSE and vice-versa. As the OTC became more reliable due to computer and communication advances, the ASE became third in importance.

4) **Regional Exchanges**

Smaller exchanges, called regional exchanges, are located in places like Boston, San

San Francisco's Pacific Coast Stock Exchange

Francisco, Detroit, and Philadelphia. They trade local, national, and international stocks. The Pacific Coast Exchange, PCE or "The P-Cos," is located in San Francisco and Los Angeles. Prices throughout the day are the same at the PCE and the NYSE, though the PCE trades later than the NYSE. It opens at 7 a.m. Pacific Standard Time and closes at 1:30 p.m. Pacific Standard Time (or 4:30 Eastern Standard Time). Stocks traded on both exchanges could have different day-end prices. Prices throughout the day are determined by the NYSE because it's so much bigger and more powerful.

When the floor trader (for your brokerage house) receives your Ford order, he/she finds (and places the order with) a Ford specialist. Specialists trade a special group of stocks for their firms. Specialists keep lists of trade orders and match buy orders with sell orders. If prices don't match, trades don't take place. When trades happen, specialists hand them to the exchange's processing department. This department processes trades on computer terminals nationwide. Specialists tell traders when trades happen. Someone then calls your brokerage firm telling your broker the trade happened. Your broker then calls you. In a few days you receive a "confirm" slip verifying the trade. You're now, undeniably, the owner of 100 shares of Ford Motor Corporation.

The Securities and Exchange Commission--SEC

Until 1933, many people made millions by engaging in unethical trading practices. The Securities Exchange Acts of 1933 and 1934 protect investors from illegal and unethical trading practices. The Securities and Exchange Commission (SEC) serves as a watchdog over the exchanges and their players. It enforces securities laws. The SEC can close entire exchanges, but--so far--has never had to.

Insider trading, trading securities with knowledge unavailable to the public, is a common securities crime. Suppose your father is on the board of directors of an oil company that recently struck oil in Montana. When the news hits the public, the stock skyrockets. Trading stock before the public knows about the wells is called insider trading (for you, or him, or anyone else he tells). This is cheating.

If the stock rises, you'll probably be caught and sent to court. If you're found guilty, a fine, suspension of securities trading, and even a jail sentence can be imposed. The SEC has put more security and faith in the investment industry.

CHAPTER 4

WHY BOND PRICES
RISE AND FALL

Why would a book about stocks cover bonds first? The answer is that bonds are simpler to understand and they affect stocks. There are also fewer things to worry about with bonds than with stocks. What makes the bond market move? Before we can understand this, we need to learn more about it.

Bonds are loans to corporations or the government. Bonds are usually issued at face or par value. Bond issuers will repay this amount (usually $1000) to bond owners at maturity (when the bond's life is over). Bond "coupons" are specified interest payments, usually made twice a year. The coupon rate is the interest rate when the bond was first issued. If we bought $1000 bonds with 10% coupons maturing in 10 years, they'd pay $100 annually (10% of $1000 = $100) for 10 years.

Figure 7-1
BELL TELEPHONE COMPANY BOND

A Fully Registered Bond

49

After 10 years we would be repaid par value, or $1000, from the bond issuers.

Where Are Bonds Traded?

Bonds have markets like stocks. There are three major bond markets. Most bonds trade over-the-counter. They're traded from broker to broker like the OTC exchange. Brokers use a system of computers like NASDAQ, National Association of Securities Dealers Automated Quotes, linking all bond-selling brokers nationwide. The next largest bond market is in New York. It's only a short walk from the NYSE. The third bond market is the American Stock Exchange. The ASE trades mostly stocks, but is also a small bond exchange. Prices for bonds on these exchanges are available in most major newspapers.

Corporate bonds trade less than stocks. Usually low-volume securities cost more to trade because traders make less. Traders have to charge more per bond to make money. Since most corporate bonds trade in low volumes, it costs investors more to trade them--a sham. Also, because they don't trade much, they're not very liquid (how easily a security can be exchanged for cash)--double sham! Government bonds are very liquid.

Now for the real thing. There are three influences on a bond's value and price: the first two are very important to understand before buying any security. These are:

- Interest rates
- Supply and demand
- The bond's credit rating

1) **Interest Rates**

Changing interest rates make bond prices rise and fall. Let's use some examples to see why. Suppose current interest rates are 5% for 10-year corporate bonds from ABC Corporation. Bonds bought from this company tomorrow would cost $1000 (par value), have a 5% coupon (or interest rate), and would mature in 10 years. ABC Corporation pays bond owners $50 (5% of $1000 = $50) annually for 10 years. At maturity, ABC Corporation repays bond owners $1000. If interest rates go to 10%, you could buy bonds from ABC Corporation with the same maturity paying bond owners $100 annually (10% of $1000 = $100). People don't want to buy bonds paying $50 annually when they could buy the same bonds that pay $100 annually. The 5% bond's price will fall--until its price is low enough that the overall investment yields 10%. Even though it seems backwards, buy when you think interest rates will fall and sell when you think they will rise.

BUY HIGH, SELL LOW

Likewise, if interest rates were 10% when a bond was issued, it would pay $100 annually. If interest rates then fell to 5%, new bonds would only pay $50 annually. This makes the old 10% bonds, paying $100 per year, more attractive. People would rather buy them, driving the old bond's price up. Our examples show that when interest rates fell, bonds became more valuable and when interest rates rose, bonds became less valuable. That's a hard investment idea for people to understand. The idea is to buy when interest rates are high and sell when interest rates are low.

The longer bonds have until maturity, the more effect changing interest rates will have on them. Short-term bond prices are affected by changing interest rates less than long-term bond prices. To understand this, let's use an example where the bonds are from the same company and have the same par value, but have different maturity dates. A two-year bond is safer than a 20-year bond because monies are tied up for only two years instead of 20. Remember, bond values rise and fall-- like stocks. If you bought the two-year bond, even if interest rates hit the roof, you'd still get your money back in two years. It might be a bad investment for two years but, if it were a 20-year bond, you'd be HURTING for a long time. This is why, when interest rates change, long-term bonds rise and fall more than short-term bonds.

2) **Supply and Demand**

The next question rushing into your brain could be, "Well, why do interest rates rise and fall?" Remember, interest is the cost of borrowing money. Like other things in our capitalist economy, supply and demand for money determines interest rates. When people want to borrow money because the cost of borrowing money is cheap, interest rates rise. Conversely, when people don't want to borrow money because the cost of borrowing money is too expensive, interest rates fall. When do people borrow money, forcing interest rates up? People borrow lots of money when interest rates are cheap or when they want to expand their businesses or buy homes. There's no sure way to tell when people are going to build houses and expand businesses, so there's no sure way to tell which way interest rates are headed.

3) **Credit Ratings**

Bonds have credit ratings just like people. Credit ratings are determined by prestigious research firms like Standard & Poor's and Moody's. These firms study companies' solvency--their "ability to pay debts." Bonds of large, stable, and very solvent companies with lots of earnings have good credit ratings. Conversely, small debt-ridden companies' bonds have poor credit ratings. The best to worst credit ratings are "AAA" to "D." Studies show a bond's credit rating affects its price. A good credit rating may allow one company to pay as little as 7% interest because there's little risk, where a bad credit rating may force another risky company to pay a higher interest rate, like 12%.

Interest rates and credit ratings affect bond prices. These factors determine a bond's popularity. If everyone wants a popular bond, its price rises--supply and demand. When there's high demand and low supply--prices rise. If bonds aren't popular and there's lots of supply--prices will fall. So, bond popularity (availability and attractiveness--supply and demand) also determines bond prices.

The most important thing to know about bonds and interest rates is: when interest rates are high, the bond markets and stock markets will be down.

BUY BONDS WHEN RATES ARE HIGH AND YOU THINK THEY WILL FALL, AND SELL WHEN RATES ARE LOW AND YOU THINK THEY WILL RISE.

CHAPTER 5

WHY THE STOCK MARKET
RISES AND FALLS

By now, you should have a fair understanding of securities. We still need to understand why stocks rise and fall. While bonds are directed by rising and falling interest rates, stocks have many more influences determining their direction. This makes the stock market hard to understand--and nearly impossible to predict.

What exactly is happening when the stock market rises and falls? Stocks are forced up and down by supply and demand. When there are many buyers (high demand) and few sellers (low supply), prices rise and vice-versa. If supply equals demand, prices will stay the same. Stocks fall until they become so cheap investors can't resist buying. Stocks rise until they become so expensive investors won't buy. So when the market is rising, people are buying and when the market is falling, people are selling. What is important to understand is what makes people want to buy and sell.

You've probably heard the terms BULL and BEAR market. A BULL market is when the stock market rises over time. The name BULL was given to rising markets because when bulls attack, they charge using their horns to throw opponents up. Conversely, a BEAR market is when the market falls. The name BEAR was given to falling markets because when bears attack, they stand tall and fall on opponents--crushing them. Also, a bear's metabolism goes down in hibernation--symbolizing the "down market."

Have you noticed how some things happen over and over? Well, the markets do the same. They rise and fall, then rise and fall--non-stop. One complete rise followed by one complete fall is called a cycle. Cycles are measured from the bottom of two consecutive bear markets or from the top of two bull markets. Generally, cycles last for 4-8 years. There are some important lessons cycles teach us. Look in the last chapter for *The Dow Theory*, by Robert Rhea. This book has valuable information about cycles.

The stock market doesn't go straight up in a bull market and straight down in a bear market. The market is always going up or down. Inside a bull market (a two to five year period when the market is going up) there may be a "pull-back" or "correction." This is an extended period (maybe a couple of months) where the market falls--but not back to the low levels of the bottom of the bull market. Likewise, a bear market correction occurs when the market is rising in the short term but never rises to the highs of the beginning of the bear market. There are even corrections in the middle of a day of trading. Say the market opens 50 points down and then comes back 10 points by 10 a.m. If you call your broker, he might tell you, "They're rallying the market back."

Why the market rallies, corrects itself, or just sits flat often baffles even professional investors. Since everyone invests for the future, the stock market is one big crystal ball. If everyone thinks the future looks bright, stock prices soar. However, if they're wrong and announcements are made to the contrary, the market will fall. Suppose Sears invented the "widget" and investors thought this widget was going to be in every house in the U.S. They would buy Sears stock thinking Sears with its widget is a promising investment. Sears Roebuck stock would skyrocket! But, suppose the widget turned out to be a failure, or it didn't do as well as investors thought it would. People would sell their stock and the price would fall as a result. Widgets show all; the stock market is a forecaster of the future. WHAT MOVES THE STOCK MARKET IS THE DIFFERENCE BETWEEN WHAT PEOPLE THINK IS GOING TO HAPPEN AND WHAT HAPPENS--THE DIFFERENCE BETWEEN PERCEPTION AND REALITY.

WOW! STOP--TAKE A DEEP BREATH AND RELAX

If people's perceptions of what's going to happen and what actually happens determine where the stock market is going, what gives people their perceptions? Generally interest rates, inflation, the economy's strength, and foreign markets are what people look at to predict the market's course. There are hundreds of other factors people use to predict the market--some aren't even as good as going to your astrologer for advice! Here are most of the things that affect the stock market:

- Interest Rates
- Inflation
- The Economy
- Tax Law Changes
- Politics
- Foreign Securities
- Human Weakness
- Company Specs
- War
- Earthquakes

1) **Interest Rates**

Generally, like bonds, when interest rates fall, the stock market rises and vice-versa. In fact, the stock and bond markets usually rise and fall together. Let's see why. Company ABC's earnings divided by its price is often calculated as a percentage. Its earnings are either given to shareholders in dividends or put back into Company ABC for growth. This "earnings percentage" is often thought of as an interest rate, because it's the amount Company ABC pays you or grows, or both. It's really called an "earnings-yield." If you take the average "interest rate" of the stock market, you'll find out whether or not stocks are a good deal compared to interest rates. If ABC stock costs $10 and Company ABC is earning a dollar per share, ABC stock is actually earning you 10%. Whether this 10% is paid in dividends, or put back into Company ABC for growth (since stock is ownership, if Company ABC is bigger you own more), ABC stock is earning you 10%. If present bonds are paying 5%, the 10% stock market earnings-yield looks good. If interest rates pay 15%, the stock market at 10% won't seem so great. Interest rates affect the stock market as they affect bonds. However, because there are other factors affecting the stock market, interest rates and the stock market don't always move in the opposite direction. A great example of this is after the 1987 crash when interest rates rose, bond values fell and the stock market rose.

Sometimes short and long-term interest rates move in opposite directions. In this case, long-term rates influence the market's direction. Why would long-term interest rates help determine the market's direction more than short-term rates? Even though people can trade stock quickly, they usually invest long-term.

So, long-term bonds compete with the market and influence its direction.

2) Inflation

Inflation and interest rates usually rise and fall together. Interest rates are influenced by inflation. Inflation occurs when the government authorizes the addition of money into the economy. Deflation occurs when the government authorizes the subtraction of money out of the economy. When the government authorizes the addition of money, there's more total money, but still the same amount of things to buy, and it will take more money to buy the same things--consumer prices rise. When inflation falls, the stock and bond markets usually rise.

Let's say you wanted to buy bonds. If inflation is 10% and interest rates are paying 5%, you wouldn't lend money. If you did, you'd be losing 5% when you're repaid. To encourage lending, borrowers have to pay higher interest rates than inflation. So at 10%, borrowers might pay 13%. Interest rates vary with inflation. That's why interest rates and inflation have much the same effect on the market. Your focus should be on interest rates. People over-value inflation's effect on the market. Interest rates are the real cause.

3) The Economy

When the economy does well, the stock market rises. Sounds reasonable, but why? A rapidly growing economy means lots of earnings for businesses. When companies earn lots compared to their price (giving a good earnings yield), people want to own stocks and their prices rise. This means a strong economy pushes the stock market up and a lagging economy crushes the stock market. Studying economics is a good idea for future investors.

4) Tax Law Changes

Why would a major tax law change affect the market? Because what makes the market move is the difference between perception and reality. If people think companies are going to earn $4 per share and, for some reason they only earn $2 per share, prices will fall. Tax law changes can make a company's earnings change. If a company is taxed 50% and a new tax law raises its taxes to 70%, it will earn less and its stock will fall.

5) **Politics**

Whether a democrat or a republican gets elected can influence the market. That's because democrats and republicans have different tax views. Democrats usually want higher capital gains and corporate taxes and vice-versa for republicans. If a democrat is elected, people fear taxes for both businesses and investors will rise. If earnings fall (because of higher taxes), or people think they will, the market will fall. If a republican is elected it's probably healthier for the market. The overall effect on the market from tax changes and politics is very small.

6) **Foreign Securities**

Most non-Communist countries have stock markets and securities like the U.S. Over the last couple of decades the value of all U.S. stocks has fluctuated between 35% and 50% of the value of all the stocks in the world. Markets exist in England, Denmark, Switzerland, Mexico, Canada, France, Italy, Turkey, Spain, Brazil, Singapore, Argentina, and more. Their economies work like ours. Most of the world's markets rise and fall together. But, not exactly.

Why would different markets rise and fall together? Say GM is selling at 10 and Toyota is selling at 15. If GM dropped to 5, people would sell Toyota stock and buy GM, because GM is cheaper, until Toyota reached 7 1/2. So, value is worldwide--it rises and falls together. Why wouldn't the markets rise and fall together? Some economies are stronger than others. One economy may bust while another booms. Laws and inflation rates also vary from country to country.

7) **Human Weakness**

Human weakness also influences the market's direction. When reality scares or bolsters investors, the market moves accordingly. When things are looking good in the stock market, prices are high, people get greedy and tend to buy. The market is forced even higher. When the market is lower, these people get scared and tend to sell. This forces the market down farther. This is the "perspective" factor. When many people buy or sell at the same time, the herd effect is created. Too many people want to buy when the market is high and sell when it's low. That's how beginners lose money. The idea is to stay away from the pack. These people can't help themselves. They fall prey to one of the worst human weaknesses--PSYCHE.

8) Company Specs

Can individual companies move the market? Yes. If IBM (the most highly valued U.S. company) stock falls $20 in a couple days, people will get scared. When people get scared, they tend to sell. Their rationale is "If it happened to IBM it could happen to my stock." It happened March 20th, 1991, when news revealed IBM would post poor earnings. IBM fell $12.75 and the Dow fell 63 points. Large price swings in the biggest companies can affect the whole market.

9) War

When people think there will be war, the stock market usually falls. Before a war, people are scared. There is a general feeling of insecurity and panic. When people get scared, the market usually falls. "Oh no! A war! What if we lose? I better sell my stock!" This pushes the market down. One prime example of "war fear" was when we went to war with Saddam Hussein. In the week before the war, as it became more and more clear the U.S. was going to war, the Dow fell from its price base of about 2,600 to a bottom of about 2,450. We knew we would win, but we were scared and the market showed it.

It might sound strange, but during wartime the stock market may rise because the government loads money into the economy. The nation unites, and people work hard. The economy cranks out whatever is needed to support the war effort. Because the economy grows so rapidly and does so well, companies earn more, and the stock market skyrockets. After war there is usually rapid inflation because governments increase the money supply so they can pay for the war with inflated dollars (less buying power per dollar). Inflation pushes interest rates up and stock and bond markets down. Larger wars affect the economy, stock market, and bond market more.

In late January and throughout February 1991, the stock market skyrocketed. As soon as the uncertainty of war was replaced with a solid decision by President Bush, the market knew how to react and started its rise. Only later did the ecstasy of victory drive the market further. But, wars don't always affect the stock market. For example, during the Korean War, the stock market remained unaffected.

10) Earthquakes

As with war, when people get scared, they tend to do crazy things. Some natural disasters make the stock market fall. For example, when the 1906 earthquake hit San Francisco--Wall Street also quaked. You can't always tell. The October 1989 San Francisco earthquake didn't seem to affect the stock market.

Even though bear markets are scary, the market goes up most of the time--about two-thirds of the time. Before the Gold Rush, there were thousands of grizzly bears in California. The Spaniards made the bears fight their bulls. Surprisingly, the bulls would win.

People buy stocks to make money. Since the stock market rises two-thirds of the time, the chance to make money in the market is good. Opportunities to make and lose money in the stock market are endless. The way most people make money in the stock market is to buy stocks when they're cheap and sell them when they're expensive. If you buy 100 shares of Company A at $10 per share and the price rises to $40 per share, you will have quad-rupled your assets.

Most people have a hard time buying a stock low and selling it high because when a stock is high, it's popular (remember, a stock's price is raised when a lot of people buy it). People have a hard time letting "fashionable" stocks go. Many beginners lose money in the market; they buy highly- priced popular stocks. While Company A is popular it sells at $40, but when Company A becomes less fashionable, the price could easily fall to $10. Let's face it, there aren't many 501 Jeans in the stock mar-ket, meaning always-fashionable and never-falling stocks. Even if there were, they aren't as likely to rise as much as cheaper, unpopular stocks.

CHAPTER 6

ECONOMICS

The stock market is a leading economic indicator, meaning it forecasts the economy. Remember, what moves the market is the difference between people's expectations and what really happens.

When people think the economy will do well, they buy stocks, and the market rises in advance of the economy. If they're wrong, and the economy does poorly, they will sell their stock, the stock market will fall, and expectations will be revised. The stock market moves a lot like the economy, but ahead of it. If you can foresee economic change, you'll be able to predict the market's direction.

The problem is, as time goes on, it's even harder to predict the economy. Today's professional economists can't predict the economy. The number of economists who have correctly predicted the economy is proportional to the number of investment managers who predict the market--almost none. If the professionals can't predict the market, why would we be able to? We shouldn't try.

In *The New Contrarian Investment Strategy*, by David Dreman, (pages 154-156), the futility of trying to predict the market is made clear. Dreman shows that the pros can't predict the economy. Of the 32 top economic forecasting firms he surveyed before the major recession of 1973-74, only one thought there would be any economic decline. Even if we can't foresee the future, we still need to understand what's happening to the economy right now--just don't fool yourself into thinking your crystal ball works.

A quick review. Interest rates influence both the economy and the stock market. Interest rates are influenced by the supply and demand for money. Who determines the supply and demand for money? You and the rest of the country. When there's lots of demand and little supply, money is injected into the economy to quench the thirst, allowing the economy the capital it needs to grow. When there's lots of supply relative to demand, money is eliminated so that there won't be too much inflation. The amount of money in the economy is called the money supply. Who controls the money supply? The government--especially...

The Federal Reserve Board

The U.S. was a guinea pig--one big experiment in democracy and capitalism. As with most experiments, we've made some mistakes. One of these mistakes was the Great Depression. Luckily our government learned some things from the Depression. It learned, in times of real trouble, it needs to give capitalism some support. It needs to push capitalism in the right direction during the good times so there won't be such horrible bad ones.

This is what the Federal Reserve Board (FRB) does. In times of trouble, it bails out the economy by lowering interest rates. In good times, it steers the economy in the right direction by making sure that interest rates don't go too low.

The FRB, also informally called the "Fed," is a government agency--that acts like the "bank's bank." It controls the money supply by creating and destroying money. It lends money to banks, determines the interest rate it charges banks, and the interest rate banks can charge you!

Now it's time to get the important part. Remember in chapter five we talked about why interest rates affect the stock market? Since the Fed can affect interest rates, it can also affect the stock market. After a year of rapidly declining stock prices in 1990, the U.S. accepted that it was in a recession. In the beginning of the year the Fed started chopping interest rates. At the end of January, just when the war with Iraq broke out, the stock market took off--the Dow went up nearly 500 points in January and February (that's like the 1987 crash in reverse).

The stock market wasn't going up only because everyone expected to win the war, but also because the Fed had decided to cut interest rates. When the Fed lowered interest rates, it made the stock market's average earnings-yield (refer to chapter five for an explanation) look a lot better. As a result, investors bought stocks and the stock market shot up. It's really kind of scary when it happens because Wall Street gets so enthusiastic, you'd think it might be time to sell stock. It's kind of like the Fed is injecting a drug into Wall Street's arm and everyone is high.

But more is affected by interest rate cuts than increased stock market earnings-yields. If interest rates are cut, you and I and corporate America have more incentive to borrow money for things like expansion and home building because it costs less to borrow. When businesses expand and people build homes, demand is created and the economy takes off. Whenever investors think businesses will earn more money, they buy stocks (to get the future earnings at a lower price now). The Fed can end a recession and encourage the economy to grow, by lowering interest rates.

The next question you might ask is, "Why doesn't the Fed just keep lowering interest rates or at least always keep interest rates low?" The reason is because it is scared of the "I-Word"-- the big no no--inflation. Inflation hurts almost everyone; it makes us poorer because we can't buy as much with the same paycheck. It's like a pay-cut.

Inflation occurs when the economy grows too fast. It's sort of like eating. When you eat the right amount, you build muscles. If you eat too much, you get fat. If we all want to build houses and have our businesses grow, we need to buy resources and products like wood for building and oil to make more stuff. When there's too much demand for products because everyone wants to build and produce, just like at a big auction, the bidding price goes way up. Then companies need to charge more for the products they make so they can make money. This is inflation--price increases.

Inflation is measured mainly by something called the Consumer Price Index (CPI). The CPI is like a basket full of goods you and I use every day, things like tires, food, and clothes. Experts watch prices every month to monitor inflation. Every month in the middle of the month the previous month's CPI is announced by the government and the stock market reacts.

Sometimes the Fed won't lower interest rates because it is scared of the "I-Word." Too much inflation makes people angry, and angry people scare the President who chooses who runs the Fed. Sometimes the Fed has to keep interest rates high so inflation doesn't get out of control.

The problem is that just like in 1990 at the end of a very long economic boom, the economy doesn't always have enough oomph in it to keep growing with high interest rates. When businessmen expect their businesses to sell more they spend a lot on things like new factories so their businesses can produce more. But, when the economy peters out and we don't buy as much, businessmen are left paying for factories that aren't being used, and so they lose lots of money. When businesses lose money, stocks collapse. Some parts of the economy get hit first. They all fall like dominos. When businessmen are unsure of economic conditions they spend less; their reasoning is, "If we go into a recession my business is going to need more cash to make it through the hard times." People who would normally want to buy houses don't because they aren't sure whether or not they will get laid off and not be able to make payments. All this to lower inflation. Obviously the FED is very important to America. It's also getting better and better at managing interest rates as it learns more and more!

You know what causes recessions and economic expansion. You know what to look for to understand why the stock market reacts as it does. Pay attention to the CPI. Investors hate inflation because it means the Fed has to keep interest rates high to keep inflation under control. Stock market investors want lower interest rates and lots of economic expansion.

CHAPTER 7

INDEXES

What do news reports like, "The Dow rose eight points today," mean?

October 1987: "The Dow crashed 508 points today!"

What does it mean? Few people know what it really means--even people who work in the industry. When the Dow falls, the market falls and vice-versa. That's about how much most people know.

The Dow is an index. Indexes are groups of stocks that are supposed to show market levels. There are lots of indexes; some are better than others. The Dow is the most popular--but not the best. To see why, we first need to learn more about the different kinds of indexes --there are three: price-weighted, value-weighted, and unweighted.

Price-weighted

The Dow Jones Industrials Average, heard daily on radio, and TV, or found in your daily paper, is a "price-weighted" index. In it are the stocks of 30 well known companies like General Motors, Exxon, Goodyear, General Electric, and McDonald's. The Dow, like other price-weighted indexes, is simply the addition of the 30 stocks' prices. Be aware--there are problems here. Higher price per share stocks have more effect on this index than lower price per share stocks. For example, say two stocks rise 10% with the market. One costs $100 and the other costs $20. The $100 stock will have five times the effect of the $20 stock on price-weighted indexes. Let's see why. If the index started out at 120 (100 + 20) it would now be 132:

```
   Rise + Original    +   Rise + Original  = Price
[{(100 X 10%) + 100} + {(20 X 10%) + 20} = 132]
       (110)          +        (22)        = 132
```

How did it get there? The $100 stock raised the index $10 and the $20 stock only raised the index $2. Say you invested equal amounts in the $100 and $20 stocks. If the

$100 stock went up 10% and the $20 stock went down 10% you'd have the same amount of money. But, the price-weighted index would be way up because of the 10% increase in the $100 stock--making an $8 increase in the index. This is a problem with price-weighted indexes. Higher dollar per share stocks raise them more than lower dollar per share stocks. They measure price and are not an accurate reflection of reality.

Value-weighted

At any given point in time a company's total value can be found by multiplying all its shares by the price per share. That value is called a market capitalization or "market cap." value-weighted indexes--also called market Capitalization weighted indexes--are calculated by simply adding the market caps of the companies in the index. Companies with more shares and a higher price per share (often just larger, highly-valued companies), have lots of influence on these indexes. For example, a company with a $100 per share stock price and one million shares of stock in existence would raise the index $10 million with a 10% price increase.

Increase X Cost X Shares = Change
.1 X 100   X 1 million = 10 million

But a $10 stock with 1/2 million shares would raise the index by only 1/2 million dollars (or, 1/20th as much) with the same 10% price increase.

Increase X Cost X Shares = Change
.1 X 10   X 1/2 million = 1/2 million

The problem is the larger stock moved the index 20 times more than the smaller one --with the same 10% price change. You would have to invest 20 times more in the bigger company than in the smaller company for this index to accurately reflect your portfolio. Value-weighted indexes don't reflect the average investors' interests--only the interests of the biggest market cap companies. The Standard and Poor's 500 and 100 are the most popular value-weighted indexes. These indexes are popular because computers can calculate and update them easily.

Unweighted

Unweighted indexes are the hardest to understand, but most reflective of investors' interests. They are found by taking equal dollar amounts of lots of stocks and adding them--as you might do if you built a portfolio of stocks for yourself. Let's make a sample index:

```
50 shares of Company A at $20 per share  = $1000
40 shares of Company B at $25 per share  = $1000
20 shares of Company C at $50 per share  = $1000
10 shares of Company D at $100 per share = $1000
                             Total = $4000
```

This is the fairest index because these stocks affect their index equally. The only real problem with this index is that when one stock goes up more than another, it has more weight or pull on the index because there is now more money in it. Unequal dollar values mean the index isn't as reflective of the market as it should ideally be. The components need to be readjusted every day to make the dollar values of each stock equal. But, when there are 500 companies in an index, it's hard to update the index daily. The longer unweighted indexes go without being updated, the less precise they are. There are no accepted standards for how and when to rebalance these indexes. They are harder to track, even with computers, and are not too widely used. The only popular unweighted index is the Value Line Industrial Composite. It's probably the best overall market indicator, tracking 1,700 stocks on an unweighted basis.

CHAPTER 8

HOW TO FIND OUT
ABOUT A COMPANY

Suppose you find names of some stocks you like. Before you can make a good investment decision about those names, you need to learn a lot more. You need to know what the company does in detail, how much it makes ... etc. You don't want to buy something without knowing much about it. Where can you find this information and what does it mean? This is what research analysts (or security analysts) do; they analyze and research companies. There are five steps to researching a company:

- Analyze its documents
- Find info about the company in the library
- Play the sleuth at the library to discover where it fits in its industry

- Visit or talk to the company
- Contact the company's competitors, suppliers, and customers

This is similar to what the pros do when they analyze companies. Each step is an important part of researching companies. They are designed to be a learning process about the company. Anywhere en route you could find something you don't like and decide not to invest. Then you don't need to waste any more time on the company. But, if you've done these steps thoroughly and found you still like the company, you've probably done enough research to make a good decision. That's what the pros do. Of course some investors buy based on little or no information, but the more you know the better your investments are likely to be.

Analyzing Documents

Before you can analyze a company's documents you need to get them. The easiest way is to go to the library. Sometimes libraries will have larger companies' documents. If not, most libraries have *Standard and Poor's (S&P) Corporate Records*, a large six-volume reference manual containing descriptions of most large companies. Once you've found *S&P*, you look alphabetically for your company's description. Under each description is the company's phone number. You should read the description--maybe you'll learn something that will make you lose interest. Then you can move on to the next company and avoid wasting more time on a loser. But, if you like what you read, move to the next step.

Because companies want their stock to rise, they give free documents to the public in the hope of interesting potential investors. They usually have a mailing list on which you can ask to be placed. So, call the company. Make sure you sound mature; they may not be interested in sending costly material to young investors--thinking young investors have very little money. Tell them you're interested in investing and ask for these documents (some are fairly common--all are important):

- Annual report
- SEC form 10-K
- Quarterly report (get the last 3)
- SEC form 10-Q
- Proxy Statement

Annual Report

The annual report is the most common document. In it are the firm's income statement, balance sheet, cash flow statement, footnotes, and a general description of what the company does--often in glowing terms written by the company's public relations firm. As the name implies, annual reports come out once a year.

10-K

The SEC requires every company to file a very detailed report like the annual report--without all the bull. It's called a 10-K, and it contains information about things like land holdings, directors, management, detailed lines of business, competitors, and customers who make up 10% or more of sales. 10-Ks, like annual reports, cover a one-year period.

Quarterly Reports

Quarterly reports are what they sound like. They contain the same info as annual reports, for a specific 90-day period (or "quarter"), but in much less detail. The reason we get the last three is to learn about the company's recent history that might affect its future.

10-Q

The SEC form 10-Q is a quarterly 10-K-like statement filed with the SEC. It's more detailed than normal quarterly reports. If you already have the quarterly reports, you can skip through the repetitive information in the 10-Qs.

Proxy Statements

Proxy statements are notices of annual shareholders' meetings. Since shareholder meetings concern electing a board of directors, proxy statements contain important information about the board and managers who want stockholders' support. It shows the managers' salaries, how many shares they own, and other info about them. In most of these statements, there is a section called "Management's discussion of operations." In it you can read the management's opinion of how things are going. This can be very enlightening.

Find Library Info About the Company

Now that you've looked over the documents, where do you go to find more? In most medium and large size city libraries, there's more research information than in most brokerage firms. There's more in the library than *Standard and Poor's Corporate Records. Standard and Poor's Stock Guide* has recent stock pricing information: P/Es (Price/Earnings Ratios), dividends, and yields. *Standard and Poor's Daily Stock Price Record* has daily pricing from the past. Look here if you need to know the price of a stock on a certain date.

Another great way to get information on companies is through *The Value Line Investment Survey. Value Line* analyzes 1700 companies on a regular basis and gives you the current scoop, past performance and future expectations for all the stocks it analyzes. It's a good idea to always see what *Value Line* has to say about each one of your stocks. *Value Line* is available in most libraries.

The *F&S Index* is like a business-oriented *Business Guide to Periodical Literature*. It lists most of the articles about companies,

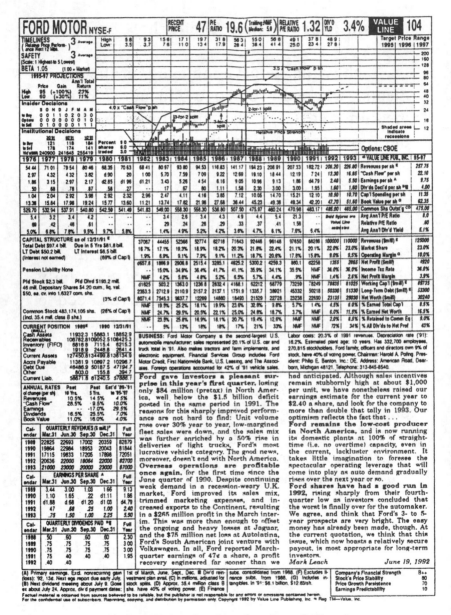

Value Line's Analysis of Ford

both in the financial press and in trade journals. If you want to learn about companies, this is a great way to do it. There's more in these articles than most investors ever learn. For example, if you're interested in a shoe company, it'll lead you to a trade journal like "Footwear News," telling you who's doing what in the industry.

Today there are lots of buy-outs--one company buying another. *Predicast's F&S Index of Corporate Change* tells you about name changes, mergers, liquidations, bankruptcies, and more. *The F&S Index* is one of the most powerful research tools young people can get their hands on--and it's free. *The Wall Street Journal Index* guides you to everything *The Wall Street Journal* has written about industries, certain topics, companies, and more. *The Wall Street Transcript* is a weekly publication covering newsletters, brokerage reports, and interviews with managers and analysts. It tells you Wall Street's opinion of the stock. Remember, don't believe the crowds. Disbelieve them. This publication tells you what the herd is mooing.

The SEC's (Securities and Exchange Commission) Official Summary of Insider

Transactions gives a breakdown of the officers and directors who are buying and selling their stock. Wouldn't you like to know if your potential investment is being bailed out by its management and directors? Then there are newsletters like *Vickers* summarizing insider transactions. They cost a bunch, but libraries sometimes have them. If they don't, sometimes they will subscribe to a newsletter if enough people request it.

The Business Index is a guide to recent articles about business persons and other subjects. It scans the articles of over 800 publications. If you want to know about all the publications in a certain field, look at *Cahners*. For example, if you want all the magazines and trade journals covering the shoe industry, *Cahners* will have it.

We've just scratched the surface. Ask a librarian for help finding these publications-- then explore--there's lots more.

Where Does It Fit Industry-Wise?

Now that you know the facts about your company, it's time to learn where the company fits in its industry. If you were a professional security analyst, you'd need to know about your companies and their industries so you wouldn't look foolish when you visit them. But even if you don't visit your companies, you should know where they fit into their world. There are three publications you'll need while you're at the library:

- *The Paine Webber Handbook of Stock and Bond Analysis*
- *Industrial Surveys*
- *U.S. Industrial Outlook*

These publications give lengthy descriptions of individual industries. You don't need to read the whole thing, just the industries you're interested in; they'll give you plenty of background. If you're looking at a shoe company, look at the sections about shoes.

Visit Or Talk to the Company

Once pros learn about the companies and their industries, they visit the companies. Because you're an individual investor, most managements won't see you. Sometimes management won't even see the pros. So, this step is limited for you. You should understand what the pros do anyway. When visiting companies, ask questions that cannot be answered with, "That information is in the annual report." Know your facts before talking to the people in charge. Investors want to be welcomed back and have management cooperate. Don't waste management's time. Help management spend time making profits, not babbling with investors about things that can be easily read in the annual report.

So, how can you have your questions answered? Call your companies and make reservations for tours--a great way to get some of your questions answered. Be sure to make a list of the things you want to know. Often shareholder relations people will answer your questions. If the company is local, go to the annual meetings; the date and address are in the proxy statement.

Talk to Competitors, Customers, Suppliers

Why would pros do this? Don't they know enough yet? No! The goal is to buy good companies the world thinks are bad. You need research above and beyond what the world in general has. Sometimes management doesn't know its stuff. It's often true of bad companies. How can you tell if the company is bad when its management isn't exactly telling you the straight skinny? Who knows the company better than people who live with it? I don't mean the employees--that's the last step. I mean the customers, suppliers, and competitors who deal and live with the company day by day.

This is an easier step for several reasons. You don't need to visit the competitors, customers, and suppliers; do it on the phone. People are more willing to give you five minutes on the phone than an hour in person. Pros cross-check information and ask several competitors', suppliers', and customers' opinions so they have a "wider view."

There are two things they can teach you. Some companies sell products because they can deliver the BEST SERVICE. Others sell products because their products are the cheapest--LOW PRICE. Some sell products because their products are made best and/or have more features--HIGH QUALITY. And then some sell lots because they deliver two or three of these qualities better than anyone else. But, most sell for only one reason. Different customers want different things--quality, low cost, or good service. Competitors, suppliers, and customers teach pros about a company's products. They also can reveal whether or not the company's management is honest. Pros learn what the company does best, worst, and to what degree of integrity.

Competitors

Sometimes competitors don't want to talk to people interested in buying their competitor's stock. Pros don't tell competitors they're interested in buying their competitor's stock. A good question to ask competition is, "When your salespeople lose sales to company A (the one you're interested in), why do they lose? When they win, why do they win? This tells what the company does best and what its competitors do best.

Suppliers

Sometimes suppliers teach the most. They know a company's history--what products the company bought and how good they were .

They also know how many of these products the company bought and how many they are supposed to buy in the future. This is a great way to look at the past and see the future. If the company's management is increasing purchases, there's probably more demand for the company's products, leading to higher sales-- a nice investment.

Customers

Pros also talk to customers. It's an easy way to get the inside scoop on companies. The names of a company's major customers (over 10% of total sales) are in the 10-K. People love to be asked what they think. Ask questions like: "How much business do you do with this company? Why do you buy the company's products (quality, pricing, or service)? What do you like and dislike about the company's products? What other people do you buy from? How much do you buy from them, and why?" This is the best time to get the real scoop from people who use the company's products. But remember it's the last step in the process.

CHAPTER 9

ACCOUNTING--A NEW LANGUAGE THAT CAN DRIVE YOU NUTS

Have you ever been to Mexico? It's pretty confusing for me because I don't know much Spanish. It drives me nuts when I try to explain myself to someone who doesn't speak English. Accounting is a foreign language if you don't know it. It can drive you nuts.

We aren't going to go into too much detail to prevent boring you to death. You'll learn just enough of the basics to properly value companies. In the process, if you're going nuts, stop, take a break, and come back to it.

Accounting is really easy--not even as hard to learn as Spanish. So kick back and don't let accounting psych you out. If you already know accounting, you might want to skip this chapter. But, before you buy stock in a company, ask an accounting whiz to make sure there aren't unusual risks you may not see. Beginning investors need only two pieces of information in order to value a company:

- Balance sheet
- Income statement

Balance Sheet

The balance sheet tells you the company's financial strength. It "balances" assets (things owned) with liabilities (things owed) and stockholders' equity. It shows what a company has and how it paid for it at a point in time. (Right now, this probably sounds like Spanish. Keep reading! By the end of the chapter, you'll be speaking the Spanish of Accounting.)

Current Liabilities

On the right side of the balance sheet, we first see the current liabilities. Current liabilities are things the company owes and has to pay within the next year. Most companies have a revolving line of credit--similar to a credit card. When the company uses its credit card, it has to pay the banks back pretty quickly.

	January 25, 1992
Assets	
Current Assets	
Cash and cash equivalents	**$13,954,770**
Marketable securities	**19,567,684**
Merchandise inventories	**18,776,959**
Prepaid expenses and other current assets	**3,226,234**
Total Current Assets	**55,525,647**
Property, Plant and Equipment-on the basis of cost	
Furniture, fixtures and equipment	**20,446,974**
Leasehold improvements	**28,582,548**
	49,029,522
Less: accumulated depreciation and amortization	**($18,445,231)**
Net property, plant and equipment	**30,584,291**
Other Assets	**595,502**
	$86,705,440

Clothestime's Assets

	January 25, 1992
Liabilities and Shareholders' Equity	
Current Liabilities	
Accounts payable	$18,874,745
Accrued sales taxes	3,508,426
accrued payroll and related taxes	4,822,199
other accrued liabilities	4,596,078
Income taxes payable	2,112,117
Total Current Liabilities	33,913,565
Long-term Liabilities	
Deferred Income Taxes	2,933,000
Other Liabilities	185,073
Total Long-term Liabilities	3,118,073
Shareholders' Equity	
Common stock, $.001 par value, authorized 50,000,000 shares, issued and outstanding	
14,551,169 shares at January 25, 1992; common stock $.01 par value, authorized	
30,000,000 shares, issued and outstanding 14,084,562 shares at January 26, 1991	14,551
Additional paid-in capital	9,934,689
Retained earnings	39,724,562
Total Shareholders' Equity	49,673,802
Commitments and Contingencies	-
	$86,705,440

Clothestime's Liabilities and Stockholders'Equity

Its credit card bills are current liabilities. All the mortgages the company will have to pay the bank within the next year are also current liabilities as well as all the other bills it owes; these are called accounts payable. As shown on the previous page, Clothestime (a discount clothing outlet) has almost $34 million in current liabilities.

Current Assets

On the left side of the balance sheet we first see the current assets. They are either cash, things that become cash within a year, or things that get used up within a year. Some of Clothestime's current assets include its cash, inventories, and its prepaid expenses (like prepaid rent). These are current assets because they get "spent" or "used" in the next year. Clothestime has more than $55 million in current assets.

A company's current assets and current liabilities give you a good feel for the company's financial strength in the next year; they tell you what the company OWES right now, versus what it now has on hand to pay what it owes. A ratio called the Current Ratio is used to give you a feel for the company's short-term financial strength. The ratio is:

Current Assets/Current Liabilities

The bigger the number the better. If a company had more current liabilities than current assets, the current ratio would be less than one. This means the company would owe more than it has to repay its short-term debts. If this company didn't earn money in the near future, it could go bankrupt. You want your company to have a solid current financial position so that it can weather life's economic storms. It's a good idea for beginning investors to consider only buying stock in companies whose current ratio is greater than 1.5. Clothestime's current ratio is: 55.5/34--just over 1.5.

Total Liabilities

Underneath current liabilities are the long-term liabilities. Clothestime doesn't have much long-term debt--good. If you add the current liabilities to the longer-term liabilities you have the total amount of debt Clothestime owes--about $37 million.

Total Assets

Just as Clothestime has long-term liabilities, it has long-term assets. Underneath the current assets, Clothestime has listed property, including land, buildings, and equipment. Total assets, listed at the bottom, are about $86 million.

What if Clothestime had borrowed all $86 million to buy its assets last month? Every dollar of Clothestime's assets would be bought on borrowed money. Clothestime would have to pay huge interest payments to the bank-- something like $8.6 million at a 10% interest rate (10% of $86 mil = $8.6 mil). But Clothestime earned about than half that in 1991. If Clothestime were that heavily leveraged (had borrowed that much) it might not be able to survive if anything at all were to go wrong, and things in life go wrong all the time. We want companies to own a good percentage of their assets in the clear so when hard times come around they can still make their interest payments to the bank. This brings us to our next topic--equity.

Stockholders' Equity

Everything a company owns was bought with money from one of three places:

- When the company sold new stock to investors to raise money
- Profits the company earned and kept for future growth
- Money the company borrowed

All the things a company has (assets at their cost) minus what it owes (liabilities) is called its "book value" or "stockholders' equity." If a company has assets that cost $12 million and still owes the bank $5 million, it has equity of $7 million (12 - 5 = 7). The equation for this is:

Assets - Liabilities = Stockholders' Equity

If we divide total liabilities by total assets, we have a ratio that tells us the percentage of liability for each asset. Clothestime has about $37 million of liabilities and about $86 million in assets: 37/86 = about 43%. This is really good. Different businesses can handle different amounts of debt. But in general you will keep yourself safe if you make sure your companies have at least $2 of assets for every dollar of debt.

Now to pull it all together. On the left side of the balance sheet are the assets. Either the company borrowed money to buy those assets or the company owns those assets in the clear. Clothestime has about $86 million in assets. Clothestime owns about $49 million of those assets and owes about $37 million on them.

$$86 = 49 + 37$$
Assets = Stockholders' + Liabilities
Equity

Or With a Little Algebra It's

$$86 - 37 = 49$$
Assets - Liabilities = Stockholders'
Equity

The left side equals the right side. This is why it's called a "balance" sheet; the liabilities plus the equity ALWAYS equals the assets--so it ALWAYS "balances".

NOW STOP AND TAKE A BREAK!!!

The Income Statement

Clothestime's income statement (on the next page) shows how much it made during specific years. Just like a balance sheet, the income statement can cover any period the accountants want it to, although it always comes out quarterly and yearly. It shows total sales, then subtracts expenses, leaving you with net income or profit. Net income is usually shown toward the bottom of the income statement. The phrase, "That's the bottom line," came from net income being shown on the bottom line of the income statement. That's the final result. A big fat bottom line is what investors want to see more than anything else.

At the top of Clothestime's income statement we see the revenues (sales). Then we see the expenses, including the cost of buying and transporting Clothestime's products (cost of goods sold), interest expense, and the cost associated with selling the products and administering the company (selling, general, and administrative). Once the accountants subtract all the expenses from all the revenues the rest is net income. On the bottom they give you some fancy information like net income per

	Year Ended **January 25, 1992** (52 Weeks)
Revenues:	
Net Sales	$258,961,741
Interest and other income	1,357,756
Total Revenues	260,319,497
Costs and Expenses:	
Cost of sales, including buying and distribution	149,815,819
Selling, general and administrative	98,816,876
Loss on disposal of property, plant and equipment	1,105,222
Interest expense	548,062
Total Costs and Expenses	250,285,979
Income Before Income Taxes	10,033,518
Provision for income taxes	4,565,000
Net Income	$5,468,518
Net Income Per Share	$0.37
Weighted average number of common and common equivalent shares outstanding during the year	14,941,307

Clothestime's Income Statement

share and the average number of shares there were on the market during the year. The key point to remember is: the income statement shows what a company makes by detailing expenses and matching them against sales. Then you can figure out things like how much the company earned for every dollar of sales (this is called its margin). Or, if there are no profits, what are they spending so much money on? Pretty key stuff.

Another important accounting fact to know is: sometimes accountants "account" differently. Accounting has lots of assumptions in it that help accountants build the numbers that go into financial statements. Accounting isn't hard, fast, and simple. Sometimes accountants use different assumptions which makes comparing the numbers like comparing apples and oranges.

Consider "depreciation." Depreciation is a way a business can spread the cost of an asset over its useful lifetime, counting a fraction of the assets' cost every year as an expense. For example, a small pizza company uses a truck to deliver pizzas. The truck is a cost of doing business--an expense costing $10,000 and is supposed to last for 10 years.

Each year it uses $1,000 or 1/10th of the truck's cost or value. Each year the company could count $1,000 as depreciation expense, subtracting it along with other expenses from the sales. At the end of the first year the company's balance sheet would show the truck as an asset worth $9,000. Or instead, if it wants, it could expense most of the truck in the first couple of years with every year's expense decreasing as time goes on until the $10,000 is used up. This is called Accelerated Depreciation.

Trying to compare a financial statement that uses straight line depreciation to one that uses accellerated depreciation is like trying to compare an apple to an orange. The footnotes in the back of the annual report show how the accounting was done. These footnotes are where you can find the REAL scoop. A poor company may have a nice looking group of statements--but the footnotes might tell a different story. Often this is the case. To make everything easy and to make themselves look better, companies often hide the bad stuff in the footnotes (which most people won't read). Every time my Grandmother buys something she says, "Read the fine print." It drives you nuts. But the same is true for investing and understanding companies. If you want to get the whole picture, you need to read the footnotes.

You need to know if the company has convertible bonds due. If they do, you need to know when the bonds are due and if the company has the strength to pay them. Companies are always suing one another for this and for that. You need to know if the company is being sued for anything substantial. Investing in Texaco without knowing that Pennzoil was suing them for jillions would have been a big, big mistake. The footnotes are where you get the real story.

If after this chapter you still don't understand, read more about accounting--it's not really that hard. One way to learn more is to pick up the phone and call Merrill Lynch. Ask them for the "broker of the day." That's the broker that gets all the new "call-in customers" for that day. Tell the "broker of the day" you are interested in investing in several companies but you need to learn more about how to read their financials. Remember, the "broker of the day" is going to want your business; he is going to be selling you hard. Ask him for Merrill Lynch's pamphlets on how to read financial statements. They are a great way to get another easy dose of accounting.

In one chapter, it's not reasonable to expect to be a certified accountant. But, you don't need to be. If you just make sure your company has a current ratio of no less than 1.5 and total assets to total liabilities of no less than 2 to 1, your company will be much more financially sound than average. If you know an accounting whiz, enlist his or her help in researching your companies. Have your very own interpreter with you--just as if you were in Mexico.

But, by now you should have enough understanding of accounting to be able to pick up a company's annual report and understand what you are reading. This is the best way to learn, by doing. After reading several annual reports you ought to be fairly fluent in accounting. Look back at the last chapter to refresh your memory on how to get annual reports. Go for it!!! And GOOD LUCK!!!

CHAPTER 10

HOW TO VALUE COMPANIES

Two different kinds of investors include:

- Value buyers
- Growth buyers

Value Buying

Buying valuable stocks sounds reasonable! What does it mean? Before we can understand what value buying is, we need to understand the trade-offs between the valuation characteristics of a company and its prospects. We will talk about this later. Put simply, value buyers buy good stocks that are real bargains. That means they are cheap relative to things like earnings, book value, or sales.

Growth Buyers

Growth buyers look for companies they believe will grow very fast and earn lots of money in the future. These companies are priced very "high" relative to things like earnings, book value, and sales. Is a $10 stock a better deal than a $90 stock? No!!! The price alone means nothing!!! What matters is how much risk is involved and how much the company earns and will earn in the future. The only way to be really good at valuing companies is to understand the risks involved, the financial info, and the company's potential. This probably seems really hard. Well, it isn't as hard to understand as it is to do.

To understand how the market values companies, you have to understand the ratios they use. Some of the ratios the market uses to value companies are:

- P/E
- PSR
- P/B
- P/R&D

The Price/Earnings Ratio--or P/E

By far the most important ratio to investors is the Price/Earnings Ratio, or P/E. If a
company's stock costs $10 and it earns $1 per
share, then that company sells for 10 times its
earnings and has a P/E multiple of 10. Remember, when your stock earns money it earns you
money, and either pays the money out to you in
a dividend or keeps the money for future growth
to help boost the future value of the stock. So,
a P/E multiple of 10 yields you $1 per $10 you
spent on the stock, or 10%. You can think of
this 10% as if it were an interest rate. The
technical term is earnings-yield (we talked
about earnings-yields in chapter five). The
P/E is just the earnings-yield inverted, or up-
side down (P/E instead of E/P). Wall Streeters
like to do everything in more complicated
ways than they need to. While E/Ps make more
sense, they all talk P/Es; so we will, too.

A P/E multiple of 10 yields you more
than a P/E multiple of 20. Why? The P/E of 20
earns you $1 for every $20 of stock or 5%
where the P/E of 10 earns 10%. It sure seems
you would rather have the investment that
earns 10% than the investment that earns 5%.

Why would people buy a stock that sells for 20 times earnings? The answer is they think the stock will do very well; they think the stock's earnings will grow rapidly. If the world thinks the company's earnings will grow at 20% every year forever, it will treat the company's stock as if it were a bond where the interest payments went up 20% every year. After a decade, the company will be earning more than $6 per year. The world will pay $20 now for every $1 of earnings (5% earnings-yield) to get the $6 of earnings in 10 years. But, in the meantime, the stock's price will go up as the earnings keep increasing. If in 10 years the company earns $6 and its growth prospects haven't diminished (the world thinks the earnings will still grow), the stock should still sell at the same P/E multiple of 20 (or 5% earnings-yield). If the stock earns $6 and sells at 20 times earnings, the stock will sell for $120 in 10 years instead of the $20 it started the decade at.

The most commonly used P/E is the "four quarter trailing" P/E, which is the current price divided by the total earnings of the last four quarters--a fancy way of saying what it earned in the last 12 months. Say a company earned

23 cents per share in the first quarter, 24 cents in the second quarter, 26 cents in the third quarter, and 27 cents in the fourth quarter. The total four-quarter trailing earnings would be $1. At a P/E of 20 the stock would be selling for $20. Say the company earned 28 cents in the first quarter of the next year. At the end of that first quarter of the second year the four-quarter trailing earnings would now be $1.05 and at the same P/E of 20, the stock would sell for $21. If the company earned 29 cents in the second quarter, 31 cents in the third quarter, and 32 cents in the fourth quarter of the second year the four-quarter trailing earnings would be $1.20 at the end of the second year. With the same P/E of 20, the stock should now sell for $24. Notice that in one year, the earnings went up from $1 to $1.20 for a 20% increase and the stock price went up from $20 to $24 also for a 20% increase.

The next question should be whether or not the P/E would stay the same. If the company's prospects remained the same and the risk seemed to stay low, the company's P/E multiple would probably go up. If I were pretty sure I could get a 20% return in the next year from buying a stock, I would buy as much as I could. Most people think 20% is pretty darn good. If you and I and all the millions of Wall Streeters who follow rumors went out and bought the stock heavily, the price would go from $24 to maybe $36. That would be a P/E of 30.

But, what happens to a company that has a P/E of 30 and then doesn't grow? Remember, the stock is like a bond that yields $1 for every $30 invested. That's an earnings-yield of about 3%. When the earnings don't grow, investors are stuck with a low yield investment and nobody wants to earn only 3%--that doesn't even beat inflation. You could do much better in the bank. In a panic, investors jump off the stock as quickly as they can. The stock might fall until the P/E is about 10. A very common time for P/E multiples to collapse is at the start of a recession. When the recession rears its head, a company can easily be taken by surprise and have its profits fall. If our company had a P/E multiple of 30 and then lost money for a couple of quarters, the stock's multiple would fall to 5 or 10. That would mean the stock would fall from 34 to about 6 or 12. Ouch!!! A double whammy--falling earnings and falling P/Es together. That's what investors call a COLLAPSING multiple! So, if you buy high-flying stocks, beware of ones that could easily lose money or grow ever more slowly.

So then, what is a "value" stock and what is a "growth" stock? Growth stocks have rapidly growing earnings and high P/Es, while value stocks have little or no earnings growth and low P/Es. What really matters is not the P/E but whether a stock deserves to be trading at that P/E. A long time ago Xerox shares were selling for $90--40 times earnings. Was that cheap or expensive? When you consider that the stock went up 13 times in the next couple of years, $90 at 40 times earnings looks pretty cheap. Likewise, Texaco selling at 7 or 8 times earnings was pretty expensive considering that it later went bankrupt. It doesn't matter so much what the stock is selling for, it matters whether or not the stock deserves to be selling for that price. We will get back to this later.

PSR--Price/Sales Ratio

What if companies don't earn much one quarter--or maybe nothing at all? Then P/Es are either high or impossible to calculate because there are no earnings. P/Es won't work in valuing these companies. A more reliable ratio can be found by using sales instead of earnings. The price/sales ratio is calculated by dividing a company's total market value (shares times price per share) by its annual sales. Say a company sells $1,000 worth of stuff one year, earns $100, is priced at $10 per share, and has 50 shares outstanding ($500 market value). This company's P/E is 5 ($500/$100) and its PSR is 0.50 ($500/$1000). These ratios show an undervalued company. If sales dropped $99 to $901 in the next year, with the same expenses, total earnings might fall to $1. If the market value stayed at $500, the stock would have a P/E of 500 ($500/$1) which is a big change, but its PSR would be pretty darn stable at .555. If you were looking for low P/Es, you would miss this stock, but not if you were looking for low PSRs. Low PSRs are 0.33 and below. High PSRs are 1.5 and above. The overall market has a PSR between 0.7 and 1. A problem with PSRs is: shareholders don't earn sales, so PSRs aren't a precise ratio for finding earnings-yields.

P/B--Price/Book Ratio

The price/book ratio is the company's market value (shares times price per share) divided by the company's book value or equity (assets minus liabilities). Positive low P/Bs are best--showing companies have lots of equity for the price. The overall market sells at between 1.5 and 2.5 times book value. The problem with this ratio is: the book value of a company does not equal what the company's assets could be sold for on the open market. Things like fluctuating real estate prices and inflation make it impossible for the historical cost of assets to be the same as what they are worth on the market today. Another common problem with this valution measure is: inventories might not be worth their original cost. For example, if a company goes out of business and is forced to sell some already poor-quality inventories, it is common for those inventories to sell for less than half of what the balance sheet said they were worth. You have to know a lot about what you are doing to be able to tell if a company is selling for less than what its individual parts are worth on the market.

The Price/Research & Development Ratio

This is my personal favorite--Price/Research and Development, or "P/R&D." There are three places where new ideas are usually created. One is in universities. Universities pay guys like Albert Einstein to just sit, think, and invent things. The second place is in some guy's garage. The last and most common is in the Research and Development Departments of corporations. Companies know, if they want to beat their competition, they need to come out with more and better products. But this costs.

I like to buy companies who have proved at least once that they can bring superior products to market before the competition. That's a sure sign of a winner. A company is not going to invest an increasing amount of money in R&D if it doesn't think the results will pay off. I like to see a company that is already investing more money in R&D than the industry average. When a company spends a lot of money on Research and Development relative to what you pay for its stock--it has a low Price/Research and Development ratio. When this company decides to spend even more on research and development, it's probably a sign that good products will be coming in the future.

If you think about it, money spent on R&D is an expense that hurts net income. Unless the world knows a "knock 'em dead" product is coming, investors will keep the stock price depressed (even if the earnings would have been good without the R&D expense). Clue: EXACTLY THE RIGHT TIME TO BUY--when the stock is relatively cheap on depressed earnings as a result of an investment in the company's future--especially when the company is good at what it does, as shown by its past performance at introducing superior products faster than its competitors.

There are other valuations like Price/Cash Flow and Dividend Yield, but you have enough for now. The key point to remember is: valuation measures like the P/E, PSR, and P/B don't mean much alone. You have to have a good feel for the company.

CHAPTER 11

RIGHT BRAIN AND
CONTRARIAN THINKING

Chapter 5 talked about why stocks rise and fall. We touched on popularity and the herd's "moo" syndrome. Let's review. When lots of people buy a stock, it rises and is naturally more popular; people like it or they wouldn't have bought it. What rises often falls. If you buy when it's too popular, it's probably priced too high and you'll probably lose money. The loser buys high, sells low (buys too popular and sells unpopular) and loses money.

The question is whether a stock deserves to be as popular or unpopular as its price. People who can look at a stock for what it is--and not what everyone says it is--are better at making this determination. A stock selling for 25 times earnings (very high) may be too unpopular. Most people never get the **buy-un-popular, sell-popular** idea down.

Many authors have written books about confusing stock market ideas. Some of these ideas are really just psychology. There are two sides of your brain. The left side, your rational side, is your $2 + 2 = 4$ facts-type side. The right side, your intuitive side, is your instincts and feelings side. Sometimes intuition is more important for investing than rationality. Lots of people don't use their instincts; they're scared of them. Others use their instincts but because of herd-type thinking, have bad instincts.

How can you stay away from popularity and use your instincts? Keep reading. What does your left side and right side mean? The left and right hemispheres of your brain are what we're talking about. When we say the market runs on fear and greed, we're talking about the right side of your brain, the emotions side.

The left side is your analytic, deductive, and fact-gathering side. Artists, philosophers, and musicians are often right-brain dominated thinkers, driven by their feelings and instincts. Engineers, librarians, lawyers, and doctors are usually left-brain driven, fact and analytical thinkers. A guy who's great in calculus could have developed very little intuition. This guy's rational side is stronger than most peoples', but he is still only using half of his brain. The same goes for people with little rationality and lots of instincts.

Which side dominates you? Everyone uses both sides, but most people are slightly more dominant on one side than the other. What side of your body is dominant? Usually, if you're right-handed, you're left-brain dominated and if you're left-handed, you're right-brain dominated. Most people have been trained since they were young to be rational thinkers and subordinate their instincts--leading to untrained instincts. This theory agrees with the fact that most people are right-handed. Other people have never trained their intuition, but let their instincts run wild. But the left-hand, right-hand idea isn't always right. A better indicator of dominance is whether you are more deductive or whether you rely more on instincts. Be honest with yourself.

Few people use an even balance of rationality and intuition. Most people are somewhat lopsided. This is good because most jobs require lopsided thinkers. Jobs involving fact calculating are often better suited to rational, deductive people. Likewise, jobs requiring tough decisions are often best suited to intuitive gut-instincts people. This is why rational thinkers are best suited to be engineers, scientists, and analysts and gut-instinct thinkers are more suited to be executives and investment managers. This is not to say that executives aren't rational or that engineers don't have intuition, but that executives have developed their guts more than their equations and that engineers have developed their equations more than their guts. Obviously, a successful engineer or executive needs some of both.

That's why you need some rationality. However, you can learn enough rationality in school from things like math and science to do the trick. (By the way, a good stats class is a very valuable tool for any investor.) Intuition and instincts are the key to decision-making and are harder to develop. They don't really have any classes that exercise your intuition. Investing requires decision-making.

Some people think you're born with intuition. Others, like myself, think it can be developed. How could we know? We do know that most top executives and investment managers are intuitive thinkers. They make up their minds correctly, and are able to do so repeatedly, without even half the facts. How? Their intuition tells them how it has to be. Intuitively, they know how the missing facts add up. Sort of like Sherlock Holmes and Obi-Wan-Kenobi all in one.

How can you develop your stock market intuition? There are thousands of ways to develop your decision-making skills. Two philosophies stand out as aids to training your stock market intuition:

- Taoism
- Contrarian thinking

Taoism

Some people claim that Taoism is a religion, but I'm not trying to preach. There is no God in this ancient Chinese "religion." It's more a philosophy of nature explaining the way things work. The Tao Teh Ching is the "bible of Taoism." There is no real translation for this name. Tao is close to meaning nature, god, the ultimate, and truth. Teh means wisdom, honor, reason, and virtue. Ching means book. The myth has it that Lao-tsu (which means wise teacher) was the keeper of the archives in an ancient Chinese city. When he was 90, he left for the hills to die. The gatekeeper wouldn't let him leave without writing down his wisdom for future generations. This is how The Tao Teh Ching, or *The Book of Tao,* was written over 2,500 years ago.

Many famous investors have used Tao to help them develop their intuition. The most famous of these is probably Dean Le Baron of Batterymarch, who manages a huge investment management firm in Boston. He is known to keep *The Book of Tao* on his desk and refer to it, often quoting it.

The Tao-Jones Averages by Bennett W. Goodspeed connects Taoism, contrarianism, intuition, and the stock market. It explains all of these ideas with real life examples. It's a true eye-opener. Learning about Taoism can't hurt you. You may just find it not only develops your stock market intuition, but that you really like the stuff.

A Contrarian Theory

Contrarianism is kind of wacky. According to contrarianism, everything is backwards. Contrarianism says it's best to do what others don't do and to believe what others don't believe--it says whatever everyone expects won't happen, so it doesn't matter much, and whatever no one expects is possible and powerful. Why? Remember the popular/unpopular example. When people like a stock and it's very popular, the price is already high. That's when it's best to sell. Most people have a hard time selling popular things--especially when lots of smart people think it's wonderful. Remember, lots of those smart people don't think intuitively; they are too rational. It's best to sell popular things and buy unpopular things--keeping you away from the pack. Contrarianism is kind of a disciplined way to be intuitive.

But, contrarianism applies to much more. My dad uses what he calls "contrarian inference" in everything both in and out of Wall Street. It's called contrarian inference because you are trying to infer what will happen or what's right using contrarianism, and it can be done on anything. He applies contrarian inference to things like political races and sports bets. It can be a useful tool for solving any problem. By practicing contrarian inference for years a person can build a formidable tool set that can be worth big bucks in the market.

If everyone thinks a stock is wonderful, it's time to sell. People buy when they think the stock will rise and sell when they think the stock will fall. If most people think the stock will fall, they're really telling you they've already sold the stock. When most people have sold stock, it's too low and will probably rise. Conversely, when people think the stock will rise, they're telling you they've already bought the stock--it's expensive. Why would they tell you before they buy it themselves? They wouldn't!

Another part of contrarianism is fear versus greed. Remember, when people are scared, they sell stock. By the time they tell you they're scared, they've already sold their stock. Conversely, when people get greedy, they buy stock. So, when you hear people getting scared, the market is probably low--people have sold. When you see people getting greedy, the market is high--people have been buying. So, you'd want to buy when people are scared and sell when people are greedy. This is just as hard as buying unpopularity and selling popularity; it's almost the same thing.

A hard thing to understand is why people buy and sell before they announce their predictions. There are some easy explanations. If you have bought stock and you convince me the stock will rise, I'll probably go buy the stock. When I buy the stock, I'm driving the price up--making you money. Likewise, if you've bought puts and you can convince me the stock will fall, I'd sell stock, putting pressure on the stock, and you'd make a bundle. Why would someone let you make money on their idea before they do? They wouldn't.

Another reason why people buy and sell before they announce predictions is: they look good when they can predict the market. Saying, "I knew it was going to happen," isn't as powerful as being able to say, "My money was where my mouth was and look at the bundle I made." More importantly, when you do what I did you're telling me you agree with me and that you think I'm pretty damn clever. Everyone likes to be agreed with and to think he's clever. By the time someone tells you he thinks something will happen, he's already in a position to profit from you doing what he said.

So, it's best to stay away from the pack. If you had done this in October of 1987 you could have saved every penny and made some. In August, at the top, people were greedy and optimistic. If you had seen the greed and the 2740 Dow, you would have sold. There were two months of pure greed in August and September. During the crash, everyone was scared. What do you do when people are scared? There's an old Wall Street saying, "Buy when the blood is running in the streets." From the Dow's low on Wednesday (just after the crash) at 1620, when everyone was scared, it rose and stabilized at about 1900. After the crash, people were still scared and the market kept rising until it hit almost 2200 in late June of 1988. Buying stock right after the crash, when people were still scared, would have made you a bundle.

The point is to stay away from herds; they trample people. Develop good instincts and use them. Be a contrarian. It's one of the hardest things to do. Human nature says to do what others do. Human nature also makes people greedy and scared. Don't listen to those emotions from other people. They don't help--they devastate. Train your instincts, have faith in them, and stay away from herds.

CHAPTER 12

A STRATEGY FOR YOU

How do investors know when to invest? Why do they buy what they buy? The answer is that most investors have methodologies, or procedures that provide perspective and help them determine what to buy and when. There are as many different strategies as there are investors. Which strategy is right for you? That's the goal of this chapter--to customize a strategy for you.

There are two main groups of investors. These are:

- Top-down
- Bottom-up

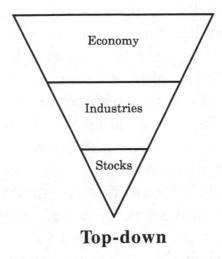

Top-down

Top-down investors first look at how the economy is doing. This takes some knowledge and intuition. If top-down investors think the economy will do poorly, they will sell stock. If they think the economy will do well, they look for the industries they think will do especially well. This is called sector rotation; they rotate from sector to sector. When they locate say 15 potential winning industries, they select the stocks they think will do well inside these industries. It's called top-down because they start by looking for economic growth, then by looking for the best industries in the growing economy, and finally by choosing individual stocks inside these industries.

135

So what's wrong with this strategy? If you can predict how the economy, specific industries, and specific stocks will do, the answer is that nothing is wrong with this strategy. The problem is: most people can't consistently predict the economy, industries, and stocks. David Dreman's book, *The New Contrarian Investment Strategy,* cites a perfect example of how difficult making such predictions consistently can be: "A survey of thirty-two major forecasters in December of 1973, for example, discovered that only one had projected any decline in economic activity the following year--1974--which saw the worst recession of the entire post war period until now."

If you can't know how the economy is going to do, which is the first step, how could you possibly do well as a top-down investor? The answer is: even though most pros use top-down, few pros do it well. Again Dreman shows 'em: "A survey of 571 of the largest pension and profit-sharing funds in the country managed primarily by banks and insurance companies for three, five, ten, and fifteen year periods ended in 1978 indicated that only 22 percent did as well as the market." Other studies have shown the same. It's tough to do "top-down" well.

If the pros can't do it, why would we be able to? The answer is we shouldn't try!!! We will have to devise a strategy that we can use without a crystal ball.

Bottom-up

There are many kinds of bottom-up investors. They start by studying individual stocks first--not by studying the economy. The most common kinds of bottom-up investors are: Black-box and Qualitative-growth.

Black-box

Even though most computers aren't black, investors have given the name "Black-box" to investors who screen for individual stocks or companies to find investments. They use parameters in their screens (boundaries for what they want) like low P/Es, low P/Bs, high compound growth, and just about anything else imaginable. The computer finds all the stocks or industries which fit the parameters. The investors then buy the stocks.

In theory, Black-box investors buy without doing any qualitative research (quality of a company, as compared to numbers). A beautiful Black-box phenomenon is that when few stocks fit the parameters because the market in general is over-priced, these investors can't find cheap stocks to buy--so they don't buy stocks.

Qualitative-growth

Then there are qualitative-growth bottom-up investors who choose stocks they think are interesting for some reason. Then, they do qualitative research. They tend to be growth investors since growth investors usually do qualitative research. The most recent famous investor whose strategy fits into this group is Peter Lynch. He says some of his best stock picks were discovered when going shopping with his family. Any time his family would find a product they really liked, Peter Lynch would research the producing company's investment potential. There can be no arguing with Peter Lynch's track record.

There are several reasons why a young investor should use a qualitative bottom-up strategy. Few young investors have the know-how or the tools to run the complicated screens run by good Black-box investors. As we saw before, you shouldn't try top-down because there are thousands of economists who have a much better chance of predicting the economy than a young investor (even then, David Dreman suggests your chances of predicting the economy are improved by simply flipping a coin, rather than listening to economists). Unless you have a time machine, you don't want to try a top-down sector rotation approach.

So what do you do? Invariably, the more companies you look at, the better you get at understanding how the market values companies. Also, if you research 100 companies, there are bound to be at least 10 in those 100 that are sure-fire winners. All sorts of lists of companies are available out there. At the front of *Value Line* in the library, they have done screens on all sorts of stocks for you and listed the results. Just start at the top of one of the *Value Line* lists you like and research your way to the bottom. In the process, you will find you either like looking at companies or you don't. If you don't, it's probably time to skip the stock market and buy a good mutual fund.

In a list of 100 stocks, there are only so many winners. In order to find winners you need to look hard!!! For every stock you end up buying, it is best to throw away at least 20. This ensures that you are being very selective.

Better yet, you could learn from Peter Lynch. For example, everyone I know who has a Vidal Sassoon blow-dryer likes it. They work. Helen of Troy actually makes them; they buy the rights to stick the Vidal Sassoon name on the blow-dryers. When I looked into the stock, I found that Helen of Troy's earnings were down because they spent a lot of money to grow, but the growth didn't come through during the 1990-91 recession. The stock was cheap and doubled in the six months after I bought it. You don't need to be a professional investor to know a good blow-dryer when you see one. Finding things you like and researching the companies that make them is one way any young level-headed investor can compete with the best of the investment pros.

Page No.	Stock Name	Recent Price	Current P/E Ratio	Time-liness	Safety Rank	Industry Group	Industry Rank
1831	WPP Group (ADR)	1⅜	1.3	4	5	Advertising	38
1186	Inter-Regional Fin'l	16	4.5	1	3	Securities Brokerage	14
1058	Advanced Micro Dev.	8⅝	4.6	3	4	Semiconductor	78
1155	Dime Savings Bank N.Y.	6⅜	5.1	2	5	Thrift	13
577	Sparton Corp.	7⅜	5.1	2	4	Aerospace/Defense	29
579	Thiokol Corp.	15	5.1	3	3	Aerospace/Defense	29
570	Moog Inc. 'A'	5⅜	5.2	3	4	Aerospace/Defense	29
1190	PaineWebber Group	22	5.2	2	3	Securities Brokerage	14
675	Alex Brown	17	5.3	4	4	Unassigned	-
2087	Pioneer Fin'l Serv.	6⅛	5.3	3	4	Insurance (Diversified)	34
1045	Safeguard Scientifics	13	5.4	3	4	Electronics	35
1183	Bear Stearns	16	5.6	2	3	Securities Brokerage	14
1105	Seagate Technology	15	5.7	1	4	Computer & Peripherals	39
572	Northrop Corp.	28	5.9	2	4	Aerospace/Defense	29
1199	Conseco, Inc.	29	6.0	3	4	Insurance (Life)	4
648	Cont'l Bank Corp.	18	6.0	2	4	Bank (Midwest)	5
605	Keystone Consol.	12	6.0	3	4	Steel (General)	74
1099	Maxtor Corp.	13	6.0	1	5	Computer & Peripherals	39
1076	AST Research	13	6.2	4	3	Computer & Peripherals	39
1084	Commodore Int'l	9⅜	6.2	4	4	Computer & Peripherals	39
790	Telefonica Espana ADR	34	6.2	3	3	Foreign Telecom.	42
427	Tosco Corp.	24	6.2	3	4	Petroleum (Integrated)	96
628	Fremont Gen'l	25	6.3	3	3	Insurance(Prop/Casualty)	20
2063	Hees Int'l Bancorp	12	6.3	3	2	Financial Services	26
1153	Boston Bancorp	27	6.4	2	3	Thrift	13
1211	Blyvoor Gold ADR	1¼	6.5	–	5	Gold/Diamond (S.A.)	–
2083	Kemper Corp.	26	6.8	4	3	Insurance (Diversified)	34
569	McDonnell Douglas	41	6.8	4	3	Aerospace/Defense	29
1188	Merrill Lynch & Co.	52	6.8	2	3	Securities Brokerage	14
1695	InterTAN Inc.	12	6.9	5	3	Retail (Special Lines)	60
1311	Curtiss-Wright	28	7.0	–	3	Machinery	46
1164	St. Paul Bancorp	21	7.0	1	3	Thrift	13
1212	De Beers Consol.	20	7.1	–	3	Gold/Diamond (S.A.)	–
557	EDO Corp.	5¼	7.1	3	3	Aerospace/Defense	29
568	Martin Marietta	53	7.1	3	2	Aerospace/Defense	29
1367	Figgie Int'l 'A'	14	7.2	4	3	Diversified Co.	43
1583	Lifetime Corp.	13	7.2	5	4	Unassigned	-
680	Raymond James Fin'l	21	7.2	2	3	Unassigned	-
1192	Salomon Inc.	37	7.3	2	3	Securities Brokerage	14
2008	Bankers Trust NY	61	7.4	3	3	Bank	11
1187	Legg Mason	22	7.4	2	3	Securities Brokerage	14
1647	Mac Frugal's Bargains	10	7.4	3	3	Retail Store	44
634	Orion Capital	36	7.4	3	3	Insurance(Prop/Casualty)	20
1606	Gitano Group	5⅝	7.5	5	4	Apparel	58
1191	Quick & Reilly Group	20	7.5	3	3	Securities Brokerage	14
638	Seibels Bruce Group	6	7.5	–	3	Insurance(Prop/Casualty)	20
2066	Loews Corp.	118	7.6	2	2	Financial Services	26
584	Whittaker Corp.	11	7.6	–	4	Aerospace/Defense	29
1582	ENDESA (ADR)	34	7.7	1	2	Unassigned	–
560	Grumman	23	7.7	3	3	Aerospace/Defense	29

Value Line List Showing the Lowest P/Es for the Stocks it Covers.

Page No.	Stock Name	Recent Price	Current P/E Ratio	Time-liness	Safety Rank	Industry Group	Industry Rank
1846	Sun Energy Partners	9	90.0	3	3	Petroleum (Producing)	59
436	Gulf Canada Res.	4¼	86.0	3	3	Canadian Energy	77
440	Numac Oil & Gas	4¼	86.0	3	3	Canadian Energy	77
866	Morgan Products	8½	85.0	3	3	Building Materials	67
1838	Louisiana Land Expl.	38	84.4	3	3	Petroleum (Producing)	59
418	Pennzoil Company	49	81.7	4	3	Petroleum (Integrated)	96
433	BP Canada	12	80.0	3	3	Canadian Energy	77
1226	Lac Minerals	7⅞	79.0	3	3	Gold/Silver Mining	57
1621	Dominion Textile	6	75.0	3	4	Textile	16
627	Cont'l Corp.	33	66.0	3	3	Insurance(Prop/Casualty)	20
681	Roberts Pharmac.	23	65.7	–	4	Unassigned	–
1080	Applied Magnetics	5¾	64.4	3	4	Computer & Peripherals	39
443	Renaissance Energy	16	64.0	3	3	Canadian Energy	77
1241	Noranda Inc.	19	63.3	3	3	Metals & Mining (Div.)	53
924	Georgia-Pacific	56	62.2	4	3	Paper & Forest Products	88
330	CRSS Inc.	9	60.0	4	3	Industrial Services	65
1566	NEC Corp. (ADR)	31	59.6	4	3	Foreign Electron/Entertn	84
619	Cominco Ltd.	23	57.5	3	3	Metals & Mining (Ind'l)	81
786	Ericsson (ADR)	23	57.5	4	3	Foreign Telecom.	42
287	Canadian Pac. Ltd.	14	56.0	4	3	Railroad	15
1862	Parker Drilling	5	55.6	3	4	Oilfield Services/Equip.	54
1229	Placer Dome	11	55.0	3	3	Gold/Silver Mining	57
1833	Anadarko Petroleum	29	52.7	3	3	Petroleum (Producing)	59
1179	United Dominion R'lty	21	52.5	3	2	R.E.I.T.	55
1258	ALZA Corp. 'A'	48	50.5	1	3	Drug	21
456	ENSERCH Corp.	15	50.0	3	3	Natural Gas(Diversified)	72
1172	HRE Properties	12	50.0	3	3	R.E.I.T.	55
897	Lafarge Corp.	15	50.0	3	3	Cement & Aggregates	61
1570	Sony Corp. (ADR)	30	50.0	4	3	Foreign Electron/Entertn	84
424	Sun Company	25	50.0	3	3	Petroleum (Integrated)	96
1859	Helmerich & Payne	24	49.0	3	3	Oilfield Services/Equip.	54
1170	Federal Rlty. Inv. Trust	22	48.9	3	2	R.E.I.T.	55
1127	Office Depot	29	48.3	1	3	Office Equip & Supplies	27
895	Florida Rock	25	48.1	3	3	Cement & Aggregates	61
1266	IVAX Corp.	24	48.0	3	3	Drug	21
145	Kollmorgen Corp.	4¾	48.0	3	4	Precision Instrument	68
1251	Lyondell Petrochemical	24	48.0	4	3	Chemical (Basic)	91
1302	Albany Int'l 'A'	14	46.7	5	3	Machinery	46
756	Centel Corp.	30	46.2	–	3	Telecom. Services	76
1803	Playboy Enterprises 'B'	7¼	45.6	2	3	Publishing	24
1061	Cypress Semiconductor	9⅛	45.5	5	3	Semiconductor	78
771	Telephone & Data	34	45.3	4	3	Telecom. Services	76
388	Turner Broadc. 'B'	18	45.0	3	4	Broadcasting/Cable TV	32
224	Medco Containment	35	44.9	2	3	Medical Supplies	66
1066	Micron Technology	17	44.7	3	4	Semiconductor	78
888	Home Depot	49	44.5	1	3	Retail Building Supply	37
1852	Baker Hughes	23	44.2	3	3	Oilfield Services/Equip.	54
1230	Teck Corp. 'B'	22	44.0	3	3	Gold/Silver Mining	57
1575	Canadian Imperial Bk	28	43.8	5	3	Bank (Canadian)	98
267	Carolina Freight	13	43.3	5	3	Trucking/Transp. Leasing	19

Value Line List Showing the Highest P/Es for the Stocks it Covers.

How To Lower Your Risk

The four ways people can lower their risk in the stock market are:

- Discipline
- Diversification
- Knowledge
- Luck

Discipline

How can discipline lower your risk? If you own a stock that's going down and you sell, you eliminate the risk that your investment will go down further. The problem is this goes against your natural instincts. Most people want to sell a stock once it has gone up some, and hold on to a stock a little longer when it falls. This is exactly wrong. Given any group of stocks--no matter who chooses the stocks--some will go up and some will go down. This means you will make mistakes!!! The idea is to realize your mistakes quickly and sell your mistakes. People with more ego than sense end up losing. You can eliminate the risk that you lose more than 10% if you tell yourself--

before you buy--you will sell a stock if it goes down 10%.

If you buy stock for $10, tell your broker you want to put a stop-loss (a trigger that stops your losses) on your stock at $9. The stop-loss sits in the specialist's computer and automatically sells the stock when the stock goes to $9--you don't have to do a thing.

Two problems exist with this system. The first is sometimes the stock market moves very quickly. It isn't uncommon to see a stock fall 25% in one day. When it happens, no trigger in the world can save you. If the stock market crashes, you have to get out when the market lets you. But the likelihood of another stock market crash soon is very small.

The second problem with this theory is you!!! That's right, you need to have the discipline to follow through with the system. If the stock falls to $9 1/8 you need to stick by your rule and not tell your broker to cancel the stop-loss. Discipline and stop-losses are the best way you can eliminate your risk. If you lose 10% it hurts--but it doesn't kill. If you lose 75% of your money because you hold on to a bad investment, that kills.

Diversification

The pros can't put stop-losses on their stocks. They have too much money!!! Everyone can't be trading billions of dollars worth of stock at once. If they have tens of millions of dollars of a stock to trade, they can't sell it all at once. They have to stay very diversified. That way, if one stock goes way down, they don't get that hurt. It's best not to put all your eggs in one basket. When you put all your eggs in one basket, you get hurt when bad news comes out on your stock and it falls 30% before your stop-loss kicks in.

So what's the right number of stocks to own? If you are investing less than $1,000, you are pretty limited in what you can do. You should probably buy only one or two stocks and stick to larger, safer companies. You will probably pay about 10%-15% just to get in and out with a $25-$35 minimum ticket. That stinks! You should be pretty sure of what you are buying--just to break even, your stocks have to go up 10%-15%.

If you have more than $1,000 to invest, your opportunities open up somewhat. With $3,000 to $5,000, you can buy three to five stocks and keep your commission down to about 5%-6% of your investment. That's a lot better. If you have $10,000-$15,000, you will probably be able to keep your costs down to about 2%-4% of your investment and still buy five or six stocks.

Long-term vs. Short-term

A stock that goes up 100% in one year has a better rate of return than a stock that goes up 1,000% in 10 years. "How can that be?" If you double $1 in a year, you get $2. Then if you double $2 in the next year, you would get $4. Doubling $4 gives you $8 in the third year. At 100% per year you get to 1,000% (or $10) in only 3 1/2 years--not 10 years. As it turns out, 1,000% in 10 years is just over 25% compounded per year.

Since most cycles last about four to eight years, it makes sense that most bull markets last about two to four years. You may find stocks that consistently out perform the market every year for four years. But few people pick lots of those consistently. That's because there aren't very many stocks that do.

Most people want to buy stocks, have them double, and sell them the next month.

This also is extremely rare. The market doesn't work like that. You shouldn't invest simply for a few months--especially when commissions cost so much relative to how much you are investing. It's one thing to try and say whether we're in a bull or a bear market--very few people can do this right. It's another thing entirely to say where the market is going to go this month--and nobody can do that consistently. Your chances are about 50-50.

When you buy stocks, plan on sitting on them for somewhere between one and two years. This gives them a chance to prove themselves. But what's really important, when deciding whether to hold on to stocks or to sell them, is not the length of time you want your money in the stock market or the return while you have held your stocks. You bought a stock you thought was undervalued relative to its past, potential, and present valuations, and the market caught on. When the price gets to the point where you think it is overvalued relative to its past performance, future potential, and present valuations, then it's time to sell. That's what's important.

Timing

Some investors trade with only a sense of timing. They try to predict the market's direction. They buy when they think the market is about to rise, and sell when they think the market is about to fall. They trade stocks they think are typical of the market--like IBM, GM, GE, and Exxon--the big liquid ones. Liquidity means something can be sold for cash quickly. They follow the market's influences telling them the market's direction. A good sense of timing is rare. Very few people have predicted the market's direction consistently with much accuracy.

When should you buy and sell? We have talked about cycles. It's best to buy after a cycle has bottomed out and has started to make its climb.

Within a two to four year bull market there will be several large corrections when the market turns south (goes down). If you can buy when the market starts to climb out of its correction, that's best.

In between corrections is a period where the market seems as if it might either go higher or go lower. If you buy when the world is scared of a further correction, and sell when the market thinks there will be another major run-up, you will probably do well.

This requires steel nerves. But, if you think about it, everyone who is scared has already sold his stock and the market will be low. When people are telling you they think it will go up they have already bought and it has already gone up. Timing is a hard thing. In general, know that you will almost never buy a stock at its lowest price or sell at its highest. So, if you are buying, just make sure you use your stop-loss, and if you are selling don't kick yourself if the stock goes up after you sell.

CHAPTER 13

COMMON MISTAKES

Most investors don't invest wisely. Investors make deadly mistakes over and over because they don't know any better. Three common mistakes investors make are:

- Consensus thinking
- Over-your-heading
- Over-trading

Consensus Thinking

Too many people invest because "So and so told me this is a great stock." This is a common mistake and a great way to lose a bundle! If someone says a stock is great, he's already bought it. He's most likely saying the stock is great so people will buy it, driving the price up--making him money. In this book, you are learning to stay away from the pack. If someone says, "Sell--the market will fall," don't listen. Resist urges to do what others say. People lose confidence in themselves when human weaknesses like greed and fear consume them. Wise investors can resist these feelings.

Over-your-heading

Why do people invest without knowing what they're doing? Another good question is: what's the easiest way to get a million bucks in the market? The answer is: start out with $2 million!

If you know the risks involved in each investment, there is no reason why you should lose half your money unless, of course, you consciously decide to take very high risks and don't have the discipline to sell your losing investments. Most people don't fully under-stand what they're investing in and, therefore, the risks involved. Whether or not they think they understand is irrelevant--most people think they do. People get so blinded by high potential returns that they completely overlook incredibly high risks. It happens to the best. Remember, a basic rule of investing is that higher potential return means higher risk. It hits investors hard when they forget. If a risk free, high return investment existed, don't you think someone else would have already taken advantage of it? Don't try to outsmart the market--it's futile. More importantly, know the whole story before investing. Don't buy anything that's over-your-head. Buy only what you can understand.

Over-trading

Brokers make commissions from sales. If brokers convince you to trade more, they make more. Beware of brokers who try to convince you to over-trade. People should invest for long time periods. Good investors make money by making a good decision and letting the decision work for them in the long run. If you over-trade, you'll not only keep your investments from ripening fully, but you'll pay lots in commissions. There are very few good reasons for selling a stock in the short term. One is that it has gone down--a mistake was made, so move on to better opportunities. Another is that it has gone up--or ripened--to the point that other investments seem to have more potential. If you invest over the long haul, keeping your investments for years, you'll pay less in commissions. With short-term investing, it's easy to waste 2% or 3% of your portfolio in commissions per year. Even though you may have to sell a losing investment in the short run because you have made a mistake, think long-term and beware of brokers who try to convince you to over-trade.

CHAPTER 14

BOOKS YOU
MAY WANT TO READ

Why have a chapter about books? If the best investors of all time told you how they made their fortunes, would you listen? Most of the best investors have written books about their own specialties. You can learn from them. Some of the books I've included were written by leading professors who know their stuff, but most were written by proven winners. Many of these books aren't available in bookstores, but you can find most of them at any major urban library. The purpose of this chapter is to lead you to areas of interest. Let your curiosity do the walking.

Technical Analysis of Stock Trends
Robert D. Edwards and John Magee

There are two widely-accepted research and investment outlooks: fundamental analysis--analysis based on fundamental business details, and technical analysis--analysis based on the history of a stock's price. The technical belief says what happened before will happen again--the past can predict the future. Technical analysts look at past price patterns and other statistics to forecast the economy, the stock market, and individual stocks. *Technical Analysis of Stock Trends* is the bible in its field. Edwards and Magee use charts. Looking at past prices and finding cycles, or regular ups and downs, they predict the future based on the past. Although they claim it's worthwhile, even Edwards and Magee admit that technical analysis is very fallible.

Cycles are commonly accepted in the investment community. The stock market travels in cycles--ups and downs. However, just because something has happened in the past doesn't mean it will happen today or tomorrow. No scientific or academic research has ever provided any solid support to technical analysis, but it's widely followed anyway. If you're interested in technical analysis, this book is probably the best. It's still in print, and most bookstores can order it.

The Dow Theory
Robert Rhea

Robert Rhea was a firm believer in the Dow theory, a set of rules and corollaries about stock market cycles created by Charles Dow, the founder of the daily *Wall Street Journal* and creator of the Dow Jones averages you hear about so often. The rules are based on repetitions found in the Dow Jones averages. If this sounds like technical analysis, you're right. Because the Dow Theory explains common repetitions in the average cycle, it is commonly accepted.

Even the most devout believers in the Dow Theory admit it isn't perfect. An example is the fact that the author of *The Dow Theory* incorrectly predicted a bear market in 1926. Many money managers use the Dow Theory at least partially. Whether or not the theory is plausible as a strategy in itself is questionable. But, because the theory shows common traits of stock market cycles, it can be valuable as an investment tool--one of many to fit in your tool box. If you're interested in technical analysis or cycles, *The Dow Theory* is another classic. It can be purchased from Wall Street

Books, P.O. Box 24806, Los Angeles, CA 90024. Wall Street Books carries many old and rare books; their "Rare and scarce books" catalog is very interesting!

The Battle for Investment Survival
Gerald M. Loeb

Gerald Loeb was one of E.F. Hutton's gurus when Hutton was one of the major brokerage firms. (Recently, Hutton was merged with Shearson Lehman to create Shearson, Lehman, Hutton, now rivaling even Merrill Lynch as America's largest brokerage firm.) Loeb had the reputation as "Hutton's tycoon." He wrote several books, some of which are highly renowned. *The Battle for Investment Survival* is the best among them. Loeb covers accepted investment principles as well as some personalized theories. He suggests putting all your eggs in one basket and watching the basket carefully, not turning your back on your stocks for a second. He also suggests buying stocks that have lots of volume and are reaching new highs. Another Loeb philosophy--if a stock falls 10%, sell it and cut your losses.

His personalized views are described in a biography by Ralph Martin, *The Wizard of Wall Street* (William Morrow & Co., 1965). If you want a different perspective, this book will give you one. It reveals the lifetime learnings of a legend.

Investment Analysis and Portfolio Management
Frank K. Reilly, Second Edition

This is probably the best investment text around. Its 895 pages offer an encyclopedia for investments, and that's how you should treat it. It's an inexhaustible source on analysis, including everything from the concepts of investing to interest rate futures. This has info on just about anything of interest. Use it as an encyclopedia. It is a detailed graduate text, but it's easy to read.

The Stock Market Handbook Reference Manual for the Securities Industry.
Frank G. Zarb & Gabriel T. Kerekes

This reference manual is less of an investment strategy book and more of an in-depth explanatory manual of the investment industry. It's much more detailed and not geared for beginners--a logical second step for those interested in deeper conceptual understanding. It can be found in most larger libraries.

The Paine Webber Handbook of Stock and Bond Analysis
Sokoloff

If you like the preceding book, you might want to read this book. They're very similar. This one describes how to analyze stocks in 31 individual industries. This is one of the easiest and fastest ways to get started learning about some industries.

Reminiscences of a Stock Operator
Edwin Lefevre

Jesse Livermore is one of the best-known stock market names of all time. Livermore was a pre-World War II trader who made and lost large fortunes. In one large, risky move after another, Livermore built and blew bundles as if he were gambling in Las Vegas. He went from the high life to broke and back four times. In the good times he lived a life of fancy penthouses, yachts, wild parties, a constant stream of booze, and a continuing rotation of new and wild women. In the bad times, he was a hustler and a gambler. In the end, he was a crumpled alcoholic who had lost it all again and finally blew his brains out in the basement of a bar. If you don't speculate like Livermore, you may hold on to your money and sanity. *Reminiscences of a Stock Operator* is a fictionalized account of his life. It never uses Livermore's name, but it's commonly accepted that the story is about him. This book is probably best for what its story tells us *not* to do. It's a must-read for a trader or broker. While it talks mostly about trading, it offers a multitude of lessons to be learned by individual investors. How? Livermore made some brilliant moves and some bumbling blunders. You can learn from both. But the mistakes are where you really profit. *Reminiscences* is currently reprinted in paperback.

Common Stocks and Uncommon Profits
Philip A. Fisher

My grandfather (or Guck as he's called by his grandchildren--my grandmother is nicknamed Muck) has been a growth stock investment manager since 1932. He entered the investment industry in 1928 and experienced the Crash of 1929. Over the years, he developed the reputation as one of the best by using strict disciplines and fundamental philosophies.

His 15 principles are qualitative guidelines used to judge investment opportunities. In a recent interview on his 80th birthday, *Forbes* magazine called him, "One of the seminal figures of modern investment thinking--one of the first, if not the first, to develop the thesis that growth stocks have identifiable characteristics that make them different from ordinary stocks."

Warren Buffett, perhaps the most successful investor of the present era, calls Fisher a "giant." Buffett, a self-made billionaire who made it all investing, calls himself "85% Ben Graham and 15% Phil Fisher."

Over the years, his biggest mistakes occurred when he didn't follow his own rules. His whole investment career is one big test of his guidelines. He has made some legendary investments in his time--some returning over *4,000%*. In his most famous book, *Common Stocks and Uncommon Profits*, he lists his principles. His book was the first investment book to make the *New York Times* best-seller list. Stanford University still uses it as a required text in its graduate investment course. For someone who is interested in basic growth and qualitative investing, learning these guide-lines is imperative. Even more educational is Guck's honest evaluation of some of his larg-est mistakes, which he shares with you. *Common Stocks and Uncommon Profits* is one of the best investment books going and may very well be the best growth and qualitative book ever. [It is currently available through this publisher--Business Classics, Woodside, CA 94062.]

The Intelligent Investor
Benjamin Graham

Ben Graham is universally known as the father of security analysis. Technical analysis looks at the market's past to predict the future (with charts). Fundamental analysis involves growth, value, or sector rotation using infor-mation about the economy, industries, or indi-vidual stocks. Benjamin Graham's first book *Security Analysis* (co-written with David L.

Dodd and Sidney Cottle) covers both these strategies in a book more like a text. This book is not suggested for you until you've read some of the other books mentioned here. However, Graham is a legend. His second book, *The Intelligent Investor,* is simpler and more of a strategy book based on what he did--value investing. He didn't believe in growth investing and outright condemns technical analysis. Benjamin Graham was an investment manager who outlined what most investment managers should do. Graham is the biggest legend by far of all the authors in this chapter. To be an intelligent and intuitive investor, you need to read Graham's *The Intelligent Investor.* No well-versed investor would admit to not having read this book. It is still available in most major bookstores.

Extraordinary Popular Delusions and the Madness of Crowds
Charles MacKay

MacKay teaches you the value of avoiding the crowd. Remember the "Herd syndrome?" Lots of people decide to do something at the same time. They often do exactly the wrong thing.

Only part of *Madness of Crowds* deals with the stock market. The rest takes you through history, exploring various times when the popular belief of the time devastated people unjustly--like the "Tulip Mania," when the Dutch gave away lifetime fortunes for a soon-to-wilt flower. It instills the idea that popular beliefs can be, and often are, incredibly fallible. It shows why you always need to think like a contrarian and question whether the crowd is right or wrong.

It's available as a reprinted paperback. You can also get it from, "The Investment Centre," a retailer of rare, used, and reprinted investment books--at 21245 Sepulveda Blvd., Los Angeles, CA 90025. Get their catalog.

The New Contrarian Investment Strategy
David Dreman

David Dreman is one of the newer investment heroes. In a few years he built a multi-billion dollar investment management firm. Dreman is a Value manager. He is largely responsible for the respectability attributed to low Price/Earnings (P/E) investing.

He was one of the frontiersmen in P/E ratios. Dreman quotes studies where low P/Es were bought, regardless of quality, and consistently out-performed the Standard & Poor's 500. Dreman maintains if you buy lots of low P/E stocks and use qualitative judgment as well, you get impressive returns.

The New Contrarian Investment Strategy gives you a good idea of a theoretically perfect value manager--disciplined, rational, quantitative, and thorough. Dreman underlines the value of contrarian thinking. He shows numerous examples of professional research analysts and economists making fools of themselves. Statistically, analysts and economists as a group can't forecast the market correctly. So, remember to keep a healthy contrarian attitude.

The New Contrarian Investment Strategy is necessary secondary reading. You can find Dreman in every other issue of *Forbes*, where he writes a column on contrarian and low P/E investing.

Super Stocks and *The Wall Street Waltz*
Kenneth L. Fisher

Every other issue, when David Dreman isn't writing his *Forbes* column, my dad writes the Portfolio Strategy column. His first book, *Super Stocks,* hit the all-time 12 favorites list of *Standard and Poor's*, *Barons*, *Money Magazine,* and *Changing Times Magazine.* In *Super Stocks* my father describes the "super stock." He describes how he finds these super stocks for his clients using black-box screening, a quantitative value strategy, and then applying qualitative strategies (like my Grandfather).

In *Super Stocks* my father gives the Price Sales Ratio (PSR) its initiation to the world. He is given credit for pioneering the PSR. Using this strategy, he once realized returns of 1,500% in two years. This is a good book for anyone interested in new value, qualitative investing and fundamental analysis.

His second book, *The Wall Street Waltz,* is a better book for beginners. It features 90 colorful charts--each with its own one-page description. It's a fascinating account of interesting investment facts.

The Over-the-Counter Securities Markets
Loll & Buckley

As a complete explanation of the technical side of investing, many people use this text to help them pass the securities exam to become a broker. Use it as a research book. A "sister" learning tool by the same authors is *Questions and Answers on Securities Markets*, which is available at most major libraries.

The Dow Jones Averages
Dow Jones

What would Dow Jones write a book about? The Dow Jones averages! This book contains the Dow Jones averages since 1885. Find the stocks which were used to calculate the Dow, when they were changed, and how. If you want to study the Crash of 1929, you have the day-by-day, blow-by-blow account. If you are interested in indexes, you will learn a lot here. It's available at most major libraries.

The Big Board
The Money Manias
Amex
The Great Bull Market
Inside Wall Street
Robert Sobel

Sobel has written some of the most interesting books on stock market history. His most famous book--a true classic--*The Big Board* is a complete history of the New York Stock Exchange. It's an interesting story revealing the reality of trading in the old days.

If you like *The Big Board,* read *Amex.* It's about the American Stock Exchange. If that's not enough for you, try *The Money Manias.* It's about the modern herd-syndrome: sort of like an update to MacKay's *Extraordinary Popular Delusions and the Madness of Crowds.* Sobel talks about the great Florida land boom and slave speculation. If you become one of the many Sobel addicts, you will want to read *The Great Bull Market* and *Inside*

Wall Street.

Unaccountable Accounting
Abraham Briloff

If you liked my accounting chapter, dig deeper in *Unaccountable Accounting*. Briloff created a revolution. He proves that an annual report's statements (balance sheet, income statement, and cash flow statement) are less important than the footnotes in the back of the report.

Some seemingly good companies are "floppers" when you read the footnotes. Footnotes show all the phony baloney--differences in accounting and the stuff that isn't mentioned in the other numbers.

Some day you owe it to yourself to read this book, but first be a bit better prepared by reading at least several of the other books in this chapter.

The Templeton Touch
William Proctor

Templeton is one of the greatest modern

accomplished foreign securities market investor. Only later did Wall Streeters discover Templeton's 40-year international gold mine.

He shops countries to find markets that have the lowest P/Es. He then buys low P/E stocks in these countries. Often he buys obscure names of small companies in these low P/E countries, holds them for the long haul, and makes a killing.

He has the best long-term (multi-decade) public track record of anyone--with statistics to show he has been making long-term profits. The biography shows his practices as well as personal glimpses of the man behind them. Almost half the book is devoted to Templeton's spiritual views and his devotion to spirituality--probably of less interest to investors. It's easy to read but out of print and hard to find.

The Money Masters
John Train

This is one of the best of the newer books. Train picked what he thought were the nine most important post-World War II investors--*The Money Masters*. Each investor and his techniques are described in an individual his techniques are described in an individual chapter including biography, philosophies and business practices. Some of the nine money masters are people you have read about in this chapter:

Warren Buffett
Paul Cabot
Philip Fisher (my "grampa")
Benjamin Graham
Stanley Kroll
T. Rowe Price
John Templeton
Larry Tisch
Robert Wilson

Train compares the masters and their strategies. This is one very interesting book. It gives you a feel for the true legends. It's still in print--even in paperback.

CONCLUSION

So let's review.

When You Are Picking Stocks...

- Always research your companies before you buy.

- Learn how Wall Street values companies. Wall Street builds its expectations into a stock's price. Practice using valuation measures to value companies until you get a good feel for how Wall Street values companies.

- Remember the only thing that matters is whether a stock is better (or will do better) than Wall Street believes it to be.

- Be choosy. Throw away at least 20 companies for every one you choose.

- Remember to only buy companies with current ratios above 1.5. This ensures your companies have good short-term financial conditions.

- Also remember to only buy companies that have twice as many total assets as total liabilities. This ensures your companies aren't too heavily in debt.

- Find someone who knows the answers to your questions and ask like crazy. It's best if they know their accounting inside and out.

When It's Time to Buy

- Determining whether it is a bull or a bear market is more than half the battle. Don't buy stocks if you think you are in a bear market.

- Be patient. Wait until the time seems right.

- Don't be just another face in the crowd. If the crowd is scared and says to sell, it's probably the right time to buy. Or, buy on gloom.

Buy when the blood is running in the streets.

● Remember to put your stop-loss in at 7%-10% below your purchase price.

When It's Time to Sell

● Don't trade stocks for cash if you think you are in a bull market. Holding cash is one way lots of people underperform the market.

● Again, be patient. Wait until the time seems right.

● Sell when everyone gets greedy--that's when the crowd is thinking the market will rise.

● Remember, only sell your stock when you think Wall Street thinks the stock is better (or will do better) than you think it is.

- Don't accept a loss on a stock when you had a 20% gain. If the stock goes from 5 to 6 then starts to fall, sell as soon as it gets to 4 & 3/4.

When Sitting on Your Stocks

- Be patient. Stocks usually go up slowly. If you sell too quickly, you might miss the stock's major run (when it goes up).

- Watch your stocks daily. That's half the fun.

- Learn as much as you can before you plunk down your money.

- One way to do this is to read some of the books described in the previous chapter.

YOU CAN DO IT!

Index

I